# Joy of the World

# 31 International Christmas Devotionals

# Table of Contents

# Preface

Christmas is a time of joy throughout the entire world – not just in the West! Christians from all continents celebrate the birth of Jesus Christ despite their differing backgrounds. *Joy of the World* features 31 Christmas devotionals taken from countries from various countries in Europe, Africa, Asia, and South America. There are 31 devotionals to be enjoyed – one for each day in December.

Each entry presents a testimony of Christmas experience from a country in Europe, Africa, Asia, or South America. Every account was written following an interview with a Christian leader who is either native to that country or has extensive living experience there. That interview was then supplemented with some contextual information about each country to complete the full devotional.

Many of the testimonies within *Joy of the World* are from Africa and Asia. It may come as a surprise to those in the West that the church is flourishing on these continents. *Operation World*, a book which provides extensive information about religious profession in countries worldwide, reports that as of 2010 there were over 503 million Christians in Africa. This is 48% of the entire population of Africa and nearly 66% of sub-Saharan Africa!

Despite facing the greatest amount of persecution of any continent, the church is also increasing in number in Asia. While Christianity is not the majority religion, there are still over 368 million professing Christians. This is over 8% of the population of Asia. In Asia as well as Africa, the Christian faith is forecasted to continue to grow, too.[1]

---

[1] J. Mandryk, *Operation World* (7th ed.; Colorado Springs: Biblica, 2010), 3, 32-33, 59.

Christianity is a truly a global religion. This is well stated by Lanin Sanneh in his volume *Disciples of All Nations: Pillars of World Christianity* when he writes:

> Christianity is the most diverse religion in the world. More people pray and worship in more languages and with more differences in styles of worship in Christianity than in any other religion. Well over three thousand of the world's languages are represented through Bible translation, prayer, liturgy, hymns and literature.[2]

Certainly, the Christian faith is not merely a "white man's religion."

While there are diverse expressions of the Christian faith due to cultural differences, there are also many similarities that link Christians worldwide together. Christians worship one Lord and Savior, Jesus Christ. They read from the same Bible, sing many of the same songs, and pray many of the same prayers. Despite the diversity, there is much in common.

When common truths are shared across cultural backgrounds, they can enrich our own faith. We can see that our personal faith is not merely an expression of our own upbringing or environment. Stories from other lands can help confirm the truth of our faith. Someone else's story can also challenge us. Their testimonies can stretch us to have greater faith or aspire to higher ideals. Someone else's testimony can also help us see things from a different vantage point. By virtue of their different setting, they can help us see familiar truths in a way that we never would have seen them before.

With the growth and enthusiasm of the church in Africa and Asia, there are many more testimonies that deserve

---

[2] Lamin Sanneh, *Disciples of All Nations: Pillars of World Christianity* (Oxford: OUP, 2007), xx.

to be heard.  The stories of these believers from these continents are stretching and challenging.  They will also provide a fresh perspective on many truths at Christmas that we in the West may not see as clearly.  Many of the devotionals within this book are from these continents.

In *Joy of the World,* there are also a number of testimonies from Eastern Europe.  Christianity was suppressed during the Communist era, but it is now blossoming again in a new era of religious freedom. Traditions surrounding Christmas that were repressed for years are now being celebrated afresh.  There are also new types of Christian experience that are engaging the spiritual vacuum left by the retreat of Communism. These are also enriching.

Included as well within *Joy of the World* are some testimonies from Western Europe.  Several of the Western European devotionals reveal a struggle to interpret the Christmas story within a secular and materialistic framework. One of these stories is concerned with a major European concern, namely immigration.  Another speaks of the importance of engaging a multicultural world.  Others relate the faithful practices of Christians that are still being held by faithful Christians today.  They encourage outreach and obedience.  These experiences in diverse Western Europe, too, have something to share about engaging the world as our Savior did years ago at Christmas time.

Every devotional in *Joy of the World* is about Christmas experience in a select country.  Every testimony also highlights a different aspect of the Christmas story.  This might be an insight on something such as the wise man's journey or a reflection on the significance of the incarnation. At the end of each devotional, there is at least one Bible verse.

Each devotional then concludes with a prayer request from the country of focus.

Some readers may not know where these countries are located. There is a map of each country included for every testimony which has been used at the permission of *Operation World*. The NIV version of the Bible is featured unless otherwise stated.

Most of the devotionals find their source from students, faculty, and friends associated with Tyndale Theological Seminary located in Badhoevedorp, the Netherlands. The seminary is adjacent to Amsterdam, one of the most international cities in the world. Others are taken from those associated with Christ Church Heiloo, an international church north of Amsterdam.

I thank each one who was interviewed. Also, I extend special thanks to Marie Elisabeth Brice, Emily Coste, Laura Thomas, Katy, Möckel, Jaap and Dory Hofstra, and my wife Andrea Williams who each helped with editing this book. Henry, Abigail, and Samuel Williams each contributed their ideas as well. This book is dedicated to my children who have celebrated many international Christmases with Andrea and me.

The Christmas message truly is one that brings joy for the whole world. May these stories increase your joy at this wonderful time of year!

# December 1:

People's Republic of China –

Chinese come to Jesus

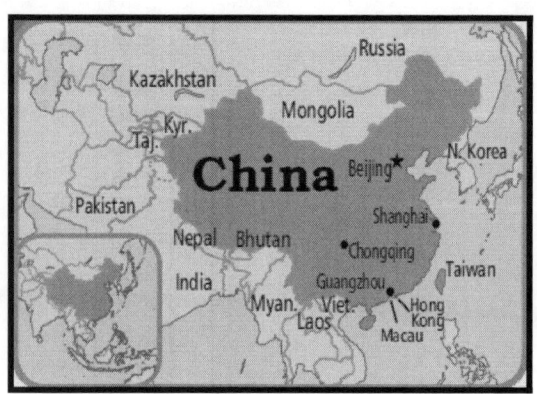

The People's Republic of China has the largest population in the world with 1.35 billion people.[3] This means that about one out of every five people in the world lives in my home country.

I come from a large city - the city of Harbin. While there are nine larger cities in China, there are still about 10 million people in my home city. Harbin is located in the northeast corner of China in the Heilongjiang province. This province is north of the Korean peninsula and is not too far from Russia. My city is about 300 hundred miles (approximately 500 kilometers) north and west from Vladivostok.

I grew up in China without hearing about the Christian faith. China has been influenced by Confucianism for centuries, and it still exerts influence today. This way of

---

[3]United Nations, "Statistics Indicators: Updated December 2010," United Nations, http://unstats.un.org/unsd/demographic/products/socind/population.htm (Accessed: June 7, 2011). This figure does not include the Special Administrative Regions of Hong Kong or Macao.

thinking has nothing to say about sin, wrong, or evil. For the Confucian, each person is created good. Someone becomes bad or evil only when that one comes into contact with evil things, but education in virtue can prevent evil. A good education in virtue will create genuinely good people, and then in turn this will make a good society.

Confucian teachings, however, are not the only beliefs within China. Communism now also exerts influence throughout my home country. Communism encourages people to devote their lives to the state. Christianity gets in the way. Because Communists are fearful of the Christian influence in China, they try to control it. Christians are advised to go to state registered churches, while other churches have to hide themselves to avoid possible persecution.

I became a Christian when I moved to the Netherlands. At Christmas time in 2003 I realized that I needed Jesus as my Savior. While I had been taught many other ways to believe throughout my life, I came to realize that my wrongdoing could not be excused by education or overcome by devotion to the state. Instead, I needed to have my sins wiped away by Jesus. He was the only one who could forgive me and grant me life.

That December I attended a Chinese church in Rotterdam, and I began my Christian journey when I heard this song called "There is a Gift." These are the lyrics translated from out of Mandarin Chinese:

> There is a gift, have you received it?
> You can't see it with eyes, but your heart can recognize it.
> This gift is waiting outside of the door of your heart.
> It is prepared only for you, others can't receive it on your behalf.

My dear friend, do you ever know?
The baby who was born in a manger has come especially for you.
My dear friend, do you ever understand?
This best gift is the Son of God, Lord Jesus.

Chorus:

Life is short, time is passing by.
If you don't take the gift as precious now,
you may not have another chance to receive it tomorrow.
Though the gift is good,
if you don't want it, how can you receive it?
How can you receive it?

Paul writes about the gift that Jesus gives us in this way in 2 Corinthians 5:21. The verse says, "God made him who had no sin to be sin for us, so that in him we might become the righteousness of God." Then in Romans 10:9-11 he writes,

> "... if you confess with your mouth that Jesus is Lord and believe in your heart that God raised him from the dead, you will be saved. For with the heart one believes and is justified, and with the mouth one confesses and is saved. For the Scripture says, 'Everyone who believes in him will not be put to shame.'"

Have you accepted this gift? You can accept the righteousness of God by faith. If you have not accepted it, then let me encourage you to do so today.

I am one of many Chinese people finding forgiveness and new life in Jesus Christ. Some are estimating that seven percent of the population is Christian. *Operation World* has noted how difficult it is to determine the exact numbers of believers in China. They write this about the number of Christians in my country.

> Accurate Christian statistics are not available. Those listed . . . are only indicative of a remarkable work of the Holy Spirit. Various official and house church network leaders have given estimates which are used here. . . Estimates of all Christians vary from 30 million to 150 million.[4]

When *Operation World* gave its best estimate in 2010, it stated that there are over 105 million Christians in China.[5] Some describe what is happening in China as a revival.

A large majority, possibly 80 million, are meeting in unregistered house churches.[6] These churches are not recognized by the government, and many meet in fear that they will be discovered. Some may have no pastor, and some may have only a portion of the Bible, but they still meet to worship Jesus. On Christmas Eve and Christmas Day, these meeting places will be filled with Chinese Christians who have great joy that Jesus came to earth years ago to save us from our sins. Please join me in praying for these believers this Christmas.

*A prayer request for China:*

Pray for the unregistered house church movement in China. Ask God to give them strength when persecuted, commitment for outreach, and strength in their leadership.

*Keran Wang*

---

[4] P. Johnston and J. Mandryk, *Operation World* (6th ed.; Carlisle: Paternoster, 2001), 160.

[5] J. Mandryk, *Operation World*, 215.

[6] See Operation World, "China," Operation World, http://www.operationworld.org/country/chna/owtext.html (Accessed: March 11, 2011).

# December 2:

# Poland – Waiting

Our family served for several years as missionaries in the town of Borne Sulinowo. It is a town of nearly 5,000 people in northwestern Poland.

This area of Poland has been occupied by various countries over the years. Before the Second World War, it was in Prussian or German hands. Following the Second World War, Poland was dominated by Communism. Between 1945 and 1992, the town was a secret Soviet military base and was not even on maps. While there was a peaceful transfer of power in Poland in 1989, the town of Borne Sulinowo was not transferred to Polish authorities until October 1992.

Despite the various countries that have occupied this town, Polish customs still remain. In our several years of missionary service in Poland, we observed that Christmas celebration went from the 24th – 27th of December. The most important night was the 24th of December. On that night, the Polish people would celebrate what is known as a *Wigilia* (vee-GEEL-yah), which literally means "vigil." This meal focuses on waiting for Jesus. It is an important family celebration.

During the *Wigilia*, the home and table are prepared with great attention. The mother of the family places a lighted candle in the window to welcome the Christ Child. An extra place is set for a stranger who may pass by. This is to remember that Joseph was a stranger who wandered from home to home looking for a place for Mary to deliver Jesus. Straw or hay is placed under a white linen tablecloth. This is symbolic of Mary's veil and also of Jesus' swaddling cloth.

On the table are 12 dishes. These are to commemorate each of the disciples and Jesus. In these dishes are a variety of salads, vegetables, breads, and soups. There is no meat since Poles fast in preparation and as they wait for Christmas Day. They will eat fish, particularly carp.

Before sitting down at the table, everyone breaks the traditional wafer known as an *oplatek*. This is very similar to the wafer used in the Roman Catholic Church. Beginning with the oldest member of the family, the *oplatek* is passed to the next person. Each family member exchanges good wishes for health, wealth, and happiness in the New Year. This is a deeply moving moment and often elicits tears of love and joy.

What role does waiting have in your Christmas celebration? One aspect of the advent season is that of waiting and expecting Jesus' return. Revelation 1:7 says this about Jesus who will come again,

> Look, he is coming with the clouds, and every eye will see him, even those who pierced him; and all the peoples of the earth will mourn because of him. So shall it be! Amen.

May your Christmas experience contain some expectation and waiting for our Savior to come again!

*A prayer request for Poland:*

After the fall of Communism, many in Poland dreamed of instant wealth. Now crime, violence, and immorality are rising, particularly amongst the youth. Pray that there would be a renewed search for God rather than materialism.

*Dan and Chris Defever*

# December 3:

# Namibia –

# Reflection

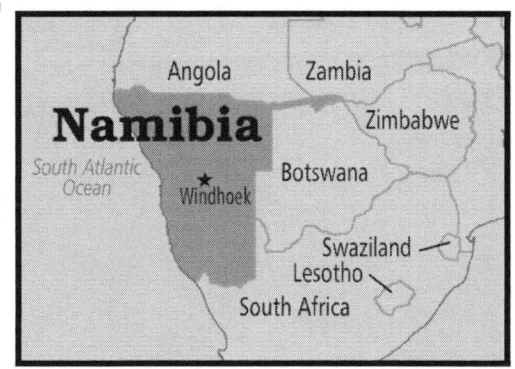

On the southwest coast of Africa and just north of South Africa is the country of Namibia. It is one of the most sparsely populated countries in the world with just about 2 million people living in a space the size of the state of Texas.

In the southern part of Namibia, the Kalahari desert and the Namib desert come together. At that point, there is the small village of Tses with about 2,000 people. It is on the one paved road that runs from the South African border in the south through to Angola in the north. Most other roads in Namibia are unpaved.

In the center of Tses, there are a few stores. There is a trading post where people can buy maize meal porridge, bread, milk, canned goods, and other basic food commodities. There is also a petrol station. In the center of town, a Namibian government office can also be found and nearby there is a police station.

Many people live here in housing made of scrap materials, predominantly corrugated iron. They supplement this with wood, glass, or cardboard. These materials are tied together with metal wire to provide shelter. At Christmas time, the average high is 98-100 Fahrenheit (35-37 Celsius). In July, the average low is 40 Fahrenheit (4 Celsius) and sometimes it can get below freezing. It can be quite cold in these houses in winter, but of course, it is hot at Christmas time.

One other notable thing about Tses is the mission station that is here. Situated alongside the town, it was built by the Catholic Church in 1927. The village formed around the mission station. Several priests live there as well as students. It is a resource to the town.

When Christmas arrives, people celebrate by going to church, often coming from far away. Some come by car, some walk, and others ride animals like mules to get to church. On an average Sunday 250 children are in church with 400 people total in attendance. At Christmas time some of the children are away, but others join us making the overall attendance still about 400. Worship will last for an hour and a half to two hours with much singing.

After church, people will go to visit with family or friends. An invitation is not necessary to come for the celebration. People come during the afternoon and evening to visit, and they may also stop in on several homes. Those who host Christmas dinner end up doing a great deal of cooking. The matriarch of the family spends a large amount of time in the kitchen cooking meat and rice. Goat would be the most common meat, but mutton and beef would also be served.

In Namibian society, people give speeches to reflect on a great day like Christmas. Leaders of families will ponder out loud in family gatherings, giving their thoughts and feelings about the day. While people in the West may give a prayer at the Christmas meal, there are certain heads of family that may speak about Christmas and its meaning for some time before friends and family in these gatherings. Their speeches will not have a time limit either. When elders of the family stand to speak, they are expected to receive full attention. Some may speak for 5 minutes and others for half an hour about the significance of the day.

Reflection is an important part of the Namibian Christmas experience. Reflection is also a part of the first Christmas story. In Luke 2:19 we read, "But Mary treasured up all these things and pondered them in her heart." While she did not speak, she thought deeply about the events that happened.

Many in places around the world do not have the time or take the time for such reflection at Christmas. They rush from one thing to another. Perhaps, this comes from advertisers and electronic media that divert attention from one thing to the next without taking the time to process what has been said or happened. May you find this Christmas some time to reflect on the importance of what has happened and is happening!

*A prayer request for Namibia:*

Namibia is a stable country, but it needs help to address the issues of poverty, land ownership, and AIDS with wisdom and determination. Pray for the church in Namibia to provide a thoughtful and caring response.

*Christian Williams*

# December 4:
# Romania – Driving out Evil

I grew up in the northeastern part of Romania in the town of Suceava. The town has just over 100,000 people. It is close to the border of the countries of Ukraine and Moldova. At one time our city was the capital of the Moldovian state from 1388-1565.

Suceava was the capital city of a famous Romanian named Stephen the Great. He ruled in this area and was victorious in many battles. He protected our area from the Ottoman Empire as well as Hungary and Poland. After his victory at a battle named Vaslui, he was given the title by Pope Sixtus IV *Verus christianae fidei athlete*: "the true defender of the Christian faith." Every time that he defeated an enemy, he built a church. Thus, there are many old church buildings in my home city.

As you can see, there is a lot of history and tradition in my city, and at Christmas time tradition continues. On the 23rd of December, the Orthodox priest comes to the home and sanctifies it with holy water. Each room must be prepared for him to do purification. He then expects an offering in return.

On the 24th of December, children come through our town and sing Christmas carols.  In response, homeowners give these young singers chocolate and money.  On the 25th, we receive gifts under the Christmas tree.  We also eat *sarmale* which is a rice dish with meat and cabbage.  For dessert we have *cozonac* which is a Christmas bread with nuts and chocolate.

On the 26th of December, a carnival atmosphere takes over.  Adults dress up in different costumes, such as a bear or a goat, and come through the town.  These symbolize evil spirits being scared away and are a reminder that God's son Jesus Christ has come to drive out evil.

The Old Testament prophet Isaiah spoke of Jesus' birth over 700 years prior to his coming.  He prophesied of the great change that would take place when Jesus entered the world.  He writes in Isaiah 9:2, 6 the following:

> The people walking in darkness have seen a great light; on those living in the land of the shadow of death a light has dawned . . . For to us a child is born, to us a son is given; and the government shall be upon his shoulder, and his name shall be called Wonderful Counselor, Mighty God, Everlasting Father, Prince of Peace.

Our Savior Jesus Christ is the light of the world.  As John 1:4-5 says, "In him was life, and that life was the light of men.  The light shines in the darkness, but the darkness has not understood it."  John 8:12 also says, "I am the light of the world.  Whoever follows me will never walk in darkness, but will have the light of life."  His presence always conquers forces of evil.  Join with me in celebrating this great tradition of our faith and the victory found in Jesus!

*A prayer request for Romania:*

Romania faces new evils today due to the legacy of Communism. Social ills such as prostitution and violent crime are on the increase. Romania's abortion rate is one of the highest in the world. Poverty is still a large problem. Pray that the light of Jesus Christ will dispel the new forces of darkness in this land.

*Ligia Manea*

# December 5:

# India –

# Fear and Joy

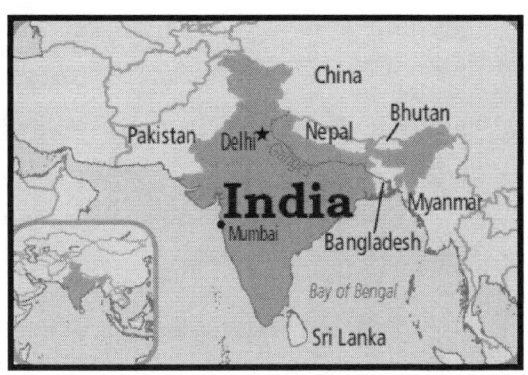

Can fear and joy go together at Christmas time? They do if you live in South Asia in the center of India. This is where you will find my city of Bhubaneswar. It is a very large metropolitan region with over 1.9 million people.

Bhubaneswar is mostly Hindu. Nearly 95% of the surrounding Orissa State is Hindu.[7] This perspective dominates the government, and it can make it difficult to be a Christian at times. The radical Hindu groups are the most dangerous. In 2008 there was some very significant violence directed toward Christians in my area. Some Christians were killed, churches were burned, and many lost their homes and property.

This continues in Orissa where Christians still live in a state of insecurity and danger. Sometimes government food supplies that should be distributed among the poor are not delivered to the Christians. In some villages Christian children are not allowed access to government schools. The former archbishop of the Catholic Church in the Orissa region named Archbishop Raphael Cheenath has said:

---

[7] J. Mandryk, *Operation World*, 436.

There is no violence, but there is no peace. About 16,000 families have no homes and Christians are not allowed to return to 20 villages unless they convert to Hinduism. In many villages in Kandhamal, Christians live with mistreatment and humiliation every day. They are not allowed to take water from the village well, collect firewood, or buy food from shops. The authorities do nothing to prevent such abuse, even if we have made complaints. Their silence is disturbing.[8]

This makes us cautious as Christians, but we still love to celebrate.

Christmas remains one of the most exciting times for Christians even with threats in nearby regions. It is a time to send cards or give gifts to friends and family. On Christmas Day, almost all families will go to church services in the morning. Afterwards there will be a time of feasting for the entire church. In the evening on December 25, Christians will gather at the church and dance, sing, act out plays, or perform comic routines. We will also act out Bible stories such as Jesus' birth.

Christmas is also a time for more intense spiritual discipline for a Christian in my part of the world. Some people like to fast during this time. They may fast for 2-3 days around Christmas. Others will devote themselves to special prayer times. Some will pray for the gospel message to reach the world or for peace. Others pray for the gospel ministry in India, especially since other religious groups are more open to the Christian message.

One Christmas I dressed up as Santa Claus with red clothes and a long white beard. Together with my friends at the church, we visited many people, Christians and non-

---

[8] Voice of the Martyrs, "India: Orissa Christians Still Living Under Threats and Persecution," (Bartlesville: December, 2010).

Christians, and then we prayed for the peace of these families. Some non-Christians are more receptive at this time of year to hear about Jesus. Non-Christians will even give food and money as a gift to the church for their Christmas celebration.

Fear and joy were a part of the very first Christmas. We read of the fear that Mary, the mother of Jesus, experienced when she heard that she was to play a role in the life of Jesus the Messiah. In Luke 1:26-33 we read:

> In the sixth month the angel Gabriel was sent from God to a city of Galilee named Nazareth, to a virgin betrothed to a man whose name was Joseph, of the house of David. And the virgin's name was Mary. And he came to her and said, "Greetings, O favored one, the Lord is with you!" But she was greatly troubled at the saying, and tried to discern what sort of greeting this might be. And the angel said to her, "Do not be afraid, Mary, for you have found favor with God. And behold, you will conceive in your womb and bear a son, and you shall call his name Jesus. He will be great and will be called the Son of the Most High. And the Lord God will give to him the throne of his father David, and he will reign over the house of Jacob forever, and of his kingdom there will be no end."

The angel told her not to fear because she had found favor with God. This Christmas, I hope that you, too, will seek favor with God. If you are feeling fear, being in the center of God's will is the best place to be.

*A prayer request for India:*

The Hindu dominated government of central India has raised tension with Christians and other religious groups. Pray that the state government may be impartial. Also, ask God to give Christians in central India courage to stand for their faith and also to promote it.

*Subal Dang*

# December 6:

## Federated Republic of Brazil – Many Aspects of Jesus

My country is known for many things. We are the fifth largest country geographically in the world behind Russia, Canada, China, and the United States. We are the largest country in South America and our borders touch every country within this continent besides Ecuador and Chile. We are also the largest Portuguese speaking country and in the top ten most populated countries in the world. Our economy is growing, and we are a member of the G20, an organization known for cooperation in economic stability.

Another face of my country is our world renowned football (soccer) team. You may recognize names like Pelé, Ronaldinho, or Robinho. Our team has won the World Cup a record five times. Some around Brazil will say about football, "*Os ingleses o inventaram, os brasileiros o aperfeiçoaram*," ("The English invented it, the Brazilians perfected it").

My home is in the northwest of the state of São Paulo. You may know that the capital of my state, the city of São Paulo, is the largest city in our country and has the strongest economy in South America. It is the second largest city behind Mexico City in the western hemisphere. Business and industry distinguish it, and the city is known for its many skyscrapers. It is the face of a developing Brazilian economy.

My village, however, has a totally different appearance than São Paulo. I am from the small town of Guararapes. As there are a number of small towns in our area, many people earn their days' wages from agriculture, harvesting sugar cane, or raising cattle. Others will work in town in the shops.

Like many towns and cities in Brazil, at the center of my town is an old Catholic Church. Brazil was colonized by Jesuits from Portugal in the sixteenth century. As the Portuguese colonized the area, they built a church in the center of the village. The church still functions as a strong community center in my area. People will celebrate feast days like St. Peter's Day or St. John's Day there. These are the so called *Festas Juninas*, for they are celebrated in the month of June.

During this time of the year, people will also gather to play Bingo at community events called *Quermesses*, which are like fairs. *Quermesses* are held by churches to raise money by selling food and tickets for prize drawings. This is an example of another aspect of life in Brazil, small town life. Many come to these events.

These June fairs have many local foods for sale. Many of the dishes that they serve feature corn, since they are celebrating the harvesting of corn at this time of year. The traditional dishes include popcorn, *canjica*, which tastes a bit like rice pudding, but made with hominy instead of rice, *pamonha*, which is akin to a *tamale*, and *paçoca,* a candy made of ground peanuts and sugar. These foods are delicious, and many make and buy these foods at *Quermesses*.

At Christmas time, people come to the church in my town to worship the baby Jesus who came in poverty. Throughout my town, people also decorate the *presepios*, which illustrates the Nativity scene, with statues of Jesus, Mary, Joseph, and the Magi. This reminds us that Jesus came as a baby on Christmas Day years ago. Many from my village identify with Jesus who came as a baby, particularly a poor baby.

While I think that this is an important thing, I believe that it is important that we remember that there is more to appreciate about the person of Jesus even at Christmas. Just as Brazil has many different faces, so the person of Jesus Christ also has many different aspects. All of these aspects are worthy of our worship even at Christmas time.

While Jesus came as a baby, it is important for my worship of Jesus at Christmas to go beyond his arrival as a weak baby. He was also a brilliant teacher who gave us wonderful teaching like the Sermon on the Mount. He also did many great miracles, helping many people. Then, he went to the cross to die for us. Following his crucifixion, he arose from the dead with resurrection power. He is alive today and is seated at the right hand of God the Father.

I can hear some of the multiple characteristics of Jesus in a passage like Colossians 1:15-20 which states:

> He is the image of the invisible God, the firstborn over all creation. For by him all things were created: things in heaven and on earth, visible and invisible, whether thrones or powers or rulers or authorities; all things were created by him and for him. He is before all things, and in him all things hold together. And he is the head of the body, the church; he is the beginning and the firstborn from among the dead, so that in everything he might have the supremacy. For God was pleased to have all his fullness dwell in him, and through him to reconcile to himself all things, whether things on earth or things in heaven, by making peace through his blood, shed on the cross.

As you come to Christmas this year, let me encourage you to see the many attributes of Jesus. He is more than a baby. The same baby who came years ago is now also supreme and rules over all creation!

*A prayer request for Brazil:*

While many from Brazil claim allegiance to the Christian faith, many are not active in their commitment and are nominal. Pray for those who are nominal to find the living, resurrected, and ascended Christ this Christmas.

*Lucia Zanetti*

# December 7:

## Bosnia-Herzegovina - Humility

My country of Bosnia-Herzegovina is in southeastern Europe in the Balkan Peninsula. We are bordered by Croatia to the north, west, and south, Serbia to the east, and Montenegro to the southeast.

Many know of my country as a result of the Bosnian war from 1992-1996. This war resulted from the breakup of the Former Yugoslav Republic. When Bosnia declared independence in 1992, forces supported by the Serbian government led by Slobodan Milošević and the Yugoslav People's Army attacked Bosnia trying to prevent their secession from Yugoslavia. This led to war breaking out all across my country. Many will remember scenes of bitter fighting, arbitrary shelling of cities and towns, and ethnic cleansing.

One of the events that attracted the greatest attention was the Siege of Sarajevo, which was the longest siege in modern warfare. There were vivid pictures sent from this siege to places around the world. The siege lasted almost four years from April 1992 – November 1995.

In the spring of 1992, the Serbs blockaded the city with approximately 18,000 men. They assaulted the city with artillery, mortars, tanks, heavy machine guns, and rocket launchers. The Bosnian forces did not nearly have the ability to break the siege. Nearly 10,000 were killed or missing in the city. Nearly 56,000 people were wounded. Many of the killed and wounded were children.

My family also suffered loss in this war. Our family home in our town of Stolac was destroyed on purpose after the Dayton Peace Accord was signed. This was a clear sign sent to us from the Croats in power in my hometown not to come back. Thankfully, the most basic structure of our house was reconstructed in the summer of 2010.

This war, however, can be traced to conflict in my area of the world for generations. The Balkan region, where my country of Bosnia-Herzegovina is found, has three major religions represented: Roman Catholicism, Eastern Orthodoxy, and Islam. These races and religions have fought and challenged one another throughout history. In the Middle Ages, there were clashes between the Serbian, Byzantine, and Bulgarian Empires. Ottomans and Christians have clashed in this area in the Balkan wars. The First World War started in the Balkans when Archduke Ferdinand was killed by Gavrilo Princip in 1914. Then, most recently, there were the clashes following the dissolution of the Former Yugoslavian Republic. Man clashes with man about his own rights and privileges.

How different it is to think of our Savior Jesus Christ and the way that he came to earth many years ago. He did not come with pride and with conflict. Instead, he came in humility to serve.

I remember Christ's humility at Christmas time. For me Christmas is the day that the great God of the universe came humbly to earth as a servant. Philippians 2:6-8 reminds me of this. It reads concerning Jesus as follows:

> Who, being in very nature God, did not consider equality with God something to be grasped, but made himself nothing, taking the very nature of a servant, being made in human likeness. And being found in appearance as a man, he humbled himself and became obedient to death-- even death on a cross!

This is one of the wonders of Christmas. The great God who created the oceans, the rivers, the deserts, and the mountains became a tiny baby. He deserved every right and privilege, but he gave them up for us. Our God came in the flesh to serve. May you appreciate Christ's humility afresh this Christmas season!

*A prayer request for Bosnia:*

During the war people were slaughtered purely because of their religion or nationality. Over 100,000 people died; a quarter of the country's buildings were destroyed. Communities that once lived together have been split apart by hatred and fear. Pray that Bosnian and world leaders will have the courage and wisdom to make peace work.

*Nenad Tunguz*

# December 8:

# England – Incarnational

# Living

In the northeast part of the Atlantic Ocean and northwest from continental Europe, you will find the United Kingdom. England is part of the United Kingdom, and it borders Scotland, which is to the north. Wales is to the west of England. The bodies of water surrounding England are the Irish Sea to the northwest, the Celtic Sea to the southwest, the North Sea to the east, and the English Channel to the south.

I come from the northwest part of England from the town of Macclesfield. It is a market town of over 50,000 people and is located in East Cheshire in the administrative district, the county of Cheshire. Macclesfield is just south of the large city of Manchester.

There are a number of old churches in my hometown such as St. Alban's Church, Christ Church, and King Edward Street Chapel. The oldest one is called St. Michael's. Some believe that this Church in combination with a neighboring field led to the name of the town. Michael's field eventually became Macclesfield. A church has been on the site where Saint Michael's Church was originally located since the time of the thirteenth century.

With Christianity so much a part of our society, many have plans on Christmas Day. A typical person from my town gets together with family. Families will have a traditional meal usually of turkey. They will also sit down in front of what we call the telly (television) at 3 o'clock to watch the Queen's speech. After that, the television rarely goes off.

Christians will go to church on Christmas Eve, traditionally for a midnight mass. These services are full of atmosphere with the singing of carols and the lighting of candles. The theme of the service is often on the incarnation. On Christmas Day some Christians will go to a Holy Communion service in the morning. This service is fairly relaxed where kids bring along their favorite presents.

My favorite Christmas carol is "O Come all ye Faithful." During the advent season leading up to Christmas, we only sing the first three verses. Then, on Christmas morning we sing the fourth verse, "Yea, Lord we greet thee, born *this* happy morning." It is at that time that the significance of the incarnation hits me.

There is concern about the Church of England at the moment with its dwindling attendance. Former archbishop of Canterbury George Carey has suggested that if the Church of England were a human being "the last rites would be administered at any moment."[9]  Cardinal Cormac Murphy-O'Connor, the former archbishop of Westminster, has said that "Christianity, as a sort of backdrop to people's lives and moral decisions — and to the government, the social life of the country — has now almost been vanquished."[10]

---

[9] Carey is quoted from Kate Fox, *Watching the English* (London: Hodder & Stoughton, 2004), 354.

[10] Gill Donovan, "Cardinal says Christianity is almost Vanquished," *National Catholic Reporter* (September 14, 2001).

As a minister now living in Amsterdam and working with a number of British people, I am eager to think about incarnational mission at Christmas time. How can we as the church be born into the communities where Christ is not present? How can we present Jesus to them? How do we listen to the cries of the people in need around us? Then, how can we seek to bring the presence of the living Lord into their midst? It is our challenge in Western Europe this Christmas to live incarnationally, presenting Christ to an increasingly secular society.

John 1:14 says, "The Word became flesh and made his dwelling among us." Another good passage about the incarnation is 1 Timothy 3:16 which says,

> Beyond all question, the mystery of godliness is great: He appeared in a body, was vindicated by the Spirit, was seen by angels, was preached among the nations, was believed on in the world, was taken up in glory.

Jesus as fully God took on human flesh to live in a world that was far from perfect. It did not even recognize him. Our challenge as Western Christians is to be like Jesus in a world that increasingly is also unable to recognize him.

*A prayer request for England:*

Pray for a renewal within the churches in England. Ask the Lord to use churches in an incarnational way in England this Christmas.

*Mark Collinson*

# December 9:

# Pakistan –

# Faith Greater than

# Persecution

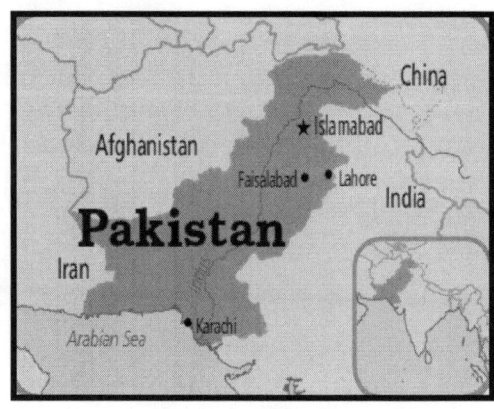

You might not think that Christmas is celebrated in a country that is 95% Muslim, but there are many Christians in Pakistan. We number just over 2% of the total population, which means that there over 3.5 million Christians in Pakistan. We celebrate Christmas, although our celebration is much more subdued now that there is fear of the Taliban.

Pakistan is in Asia. It is north of India and east of Afghanistan and Iran. The northeast corner of the country touches China. There are over 170 million people in my country, making us the sixth most populated country in the world.

Christmas celebrations begin for us on December 1. On this day Christians will begin to decorate their homes. As we make our way through December, preparation for Christmas becomes greater. Children begin to practice Christmas plays in order to perform them in the church on Christmas Eve. We also begin to buy gifts, such as dried fruit and new clothes, to give to loved ones. We will give these on or around Christmas Day.

Besides these activities, Christians in Pakistan believe that Christmas is a time to greet people and share the joy of the season. We greet people in the streets. In the past many of us would also sing folk songs in public, although now we are more fearful and cautious.

We gather for special services on December 24 and 25. On these days, we are also allowed to tell the message of Jesus Christ on TV in Pakistan. The government allows us to proclaim that Jesus, the Prince of Peace, has come since Christmas is known as a Christian day. Many Pakistanis hear the gospel message through the media at Christmas time.

As of 2001, we are less bold. Christians are afraid of Muslims because Sharia law has been implemented. Sharia law covers all aspects of human life: personal worship, commercial dealings, marriage, and penal laws. This law is very strict in Pakistan, and it is difficult for any minority other than Muslim. Under this law, people can be accused of blasphemy. If someone is suspected of saying anything against Islam or Mohammed, that person can lose their job, be thrown in jail, or even lose their lives.

There are many Christians in Pakistan who have been persecuted for their faith. For example, in December 2009 fifty Muslims with clubs and axes entered a church that was showing the *Jesus Film*. When they saw the part where Jesus was resurrected, they became enraged and began to attack those showing the film. They also damaged the film projector and burned reels of the film. This is one of many stories of persecution in Pakistan.[11]

---

[11] Jawad Mazhar, "PAKISTAN: Church Attacked Screening of 'Jesus Film,'"Open Doors, http://www.opendoors.org.nz/article/143/pakistan-church-attacked-screening-of-jesus-film (Accessed: May 14, 2011).

On Feb. 22, 2009, the Taliban attacked six churches, burned several Christian homes, burned four Bibles, and injured children in Karachi, Pakistan. Eyewitnesses reported the Taliban shouting, "Accept Islam, accept Islam.  La Ilaha Ill Allah Muhammadur Rasool Allah."  This means, "There is no god, only Allah, Muhammad is the messenger of Allah."[12]

In 2010 the only Christian cabinet member Shahbaz Bhatti was killed in Pakistan.  He was a committed Christian and was trying to reform the blasphemy law.  As his car drove through a residential neighborhood in Islamabad, he was shot by Muslim extremists.  Pamphlets from Al-Qaeda were distributed at the spot where he was pulled from his car.  The pamphlets defended Pakistan's blasphemy law.[13]

Many in the West think only of happiness at Christmas time.  For some in this world, Christmas is only about pleasure, seeing family, and eating a big meal. There are other emotions within the Christmas story.  It does have some fear in it.

We can hear fear at the first Christmas when we read Matthew 2:13-16.  This passage follows the wise men appearing reads as follows:

---

[12] Voice of the Martyrs, "Pakistan:  Six Churches Attacked," Voice of the Martyrs, http://www.persecution.com/public/newsroom.aspx?story_ID=MTEy (Accessed:  May 14, 2011).
[13]Voice of the Martyrs, "Pakistan Christian Minister Killed," Voice of the Martyrs, http://www.persecution.com/public/newsroom.aspx?story_ID=MzQ0&featuredstory_ID=MjE2&clickfrom=ZmVhdHVyZWRzdG9yaWVz (Accessed:  March 11, 2011).

Now when they had departed, behold, an angel of the Lord appeared to Joseph in a dream and said, "Rise, take the child and his mother, and flee to Egypt, and remain there until I tell you, for Herod is about to search for the child, to destroy him." And he rose and took the child and his mother by night and departed to Egypt and remained there until the death of Herod. This was to fulfill what the Lord had spoken by the prophet, "Out of Egypt I called my son." Then Herod, when he saw that he had been tricked by the wise men, became furious, and he sent and killed all the male children in Bethlehem and in all that region who were two years old or under, according to the time that he had ascertained from the wise men.

There is fear that King Herod will kill God's Promised Deliverer. Despite the fear found in the Christmas story, faith triumphs.

Please remember to pray for the persecuted church like the church in Pakistan at Christmas. As you do, remember that faith and true Christian joy still triumph over fear.

*A prayer request for Pakistan:*

Pray that amidst suffering, Christians in Pakistan may draw close to the Lord. Ask that God would strengthen them and give them courage when facing intimidation and persecution.

*Shehzahd Ohri*

# December 10:

## The Republic of Serbia – Preparation

My wife Linda and I served as missionaries in Serbia for 20 years. Serbia is a landlocked country in Eastern Europe in the Balkan region. It borders Hungary, Romania, Bulgaria, Macedonia, Albania, Montenegro, Croatia, and Bosnia and Herzegovina. There are over 7 million people within Serbia.

Most of the population is connected with the Orthodox Church, which claims over 6 million followers. There are also Muslim, Jewish, Catholic, and Baptist groups in the country. During our time in Serbia, we belonged to a Baptist church. The Baptists in Serbia celebrate Christmas on December 25, but the Orthodox Church celebrates Christmas on January 7.

There are many Christmas traditions amongst the Serbian people. Let me share with you a few. Serbs celebrate the holiday with a yule log called a *badnjak*. The *badnjak* is a young oak that is cut on the morning of Christmas Eve, and then is brought into the home that evening. This yule log would burn throughout that evening and also the following day. The family burns the log, and then also prays that God will bring his blessings during the coming year. It is customary for the first person who visits the family on Christmas Day to strike the burning *badnjak* with a poker or a branch. He should strike it hard enough to make sparks fly from it and then extend wishes for happiness, prosperity, health, and joy for the family.

Being prepared for Christmas Day is important in Serbia. During the week leading up to Christmas, many Christians in Belgrade fast from eating meat. By fasting before Christmas Day, Serbs focus afresh on receiving God's gift. The fast is broken on Christmas Eve after the church service. Serbs break this fast by eating *poedranac* which is a mixture of baked beans and onions. Meat is eaten the following day at Christmas dinner.

Christmas dinner is the most festive meal of the year. Before the table is set, it is strewn with a thin layer of straw. Then, it is covered with a white cloth, and the table is set. Dinner begins about noon, or sometimes even earlier. The head of the household will ask family members seated at the table to stand. He will make the sign of the cross, light a candle, and then pray. Following the prayer, everyone kisses each other and says, "Peace of God, Christ is Born."

Afterwards, the head of the household and another man of the family will hold special bread called the *česnica* between them. This bread was prepared on Christmas Eve. They rotate it three times, and then pass it around the table. All of the relatives will break it, and each person will take his or her own piece. A piece of the loaf will be set aside for absent family members, and another piece will be left for a stranger who might become a guest at the table. The rest of the loaf will be eaten during dinner. There is a piece of the *česnica* that has a coin in it. Good luck will come to the one who has this piece.

The meat fast is then broken later at Christmas dinner. Most in the area of Belgrade where we lived had roast pork as the main course. This pork is very tasty and is cooked by rotating it over an open fire.

Preparation is an important part of the Serbian Christmas experience. Many from the West forget about this even though it is a theme of the advent season. Is there a part of your Christmas celebration that includes purity and preparation?

Preparation comes to the forefront in Mark's Gospel. This Gospel is the only one of the four New Testament Gospels that does not include any actual details of Jesus' arrival on earth. The Gospel does begin by calling people to prepare themselves to meet Jesus.

We read the following in Mark 1:1-3:

> The beginning of the gospel about Jesus Christ, the Son of God. It is written in Isaiah the prophet: "I will send my messenger ahead of you, who will prepare your way"-- "a voice of one calling in the desert, 'Prepare the way for the Lord, make straight paths for him.'"

May you find some time during your Christmas season to prepare your heart for God's Son.

*A prayer request for Serbia:*

There are few Evangelical believers in Serbia. Most congregations are small and scattered. The suffering of the war in the 1990s has not helped. Pray for Protestant churches such as Baptist and Pentecostal churches in Serbia especially in their outreach and commitment.

*Phil Gottschalk*

# December 11: The Netherlands - A Light for Jesus

The Netherlands is located on the north and west corner of Europe. It is north and east of Belgium and west of Germany. I have grown up in the Netherlands and have spent most of my life here. Together my husband and I have been involved in church planting in North Holland for twenty years. We live in Heiloo, a town of just over 22,000 inhabitants.

The Dutch celebrate two days for Christmas – December 25 and 26. The reason there are 2 days that the Dutch celebrate each Christian holiday (also Easter and Pentecost) is because in the past they wouldn't travel on Sundays since they honored it as a day of rest. Therefore, families could travel on the 2nd holiday. Nowadays it is only handy to have two days to celebrate Christmas. One can spend the first day with one side of the family, and the other day with the in-laws, the other side of the family.

Eating together is the most important activity for these two days and can last several hours. Some families can do a fondue or "gourmet cooking" (i.e., cooking your own meat, onions, and mushrooms in tiny little pans in the middle of the table). Having a late breakfast is also special to do as a family. We enjoy eating boiled eggs and special bread rolls at Christmas time like many other Dutch families.

Most Christians will attend church at Christmas time. Christians go to church on December 25 – first Christmas day. Usually on December 26, the second Christmas day, there is some kind of celebration for children in the church who have prepared something with the Sunday school.

While many places in the Netherlands celebrate two Christmas Days, there are an increasing number of people who are not celebrating Christmas at all. Many are forgetting the significance of Christmas Day, namely that Jesus left heaven and came to earth to redeem people from their sins. While the Netherlands has been traditionally known as a Christian country, recent statistics reveal that the church is declining. Those who profess to be Christians number about 45% of the population. This, however, is a substantial decrease from the past century. In 1900, nearly everyone considered themselves Christian and went to church. Statistics from 2010 reveal that Protestants comprise 17% of the population and the Roman Catholic Church embraces another 25%. These traditional churches have been projected to get even smaller in the coming years. [14] The Netherlands is in need of the light of Jesus Christ to shine again brightly.

While things are dark in the Netherlands, there are ways to combat darkness. You can be a light yourself, pointing others to Jesus Christ. One light can change darkness dramatically. In the winter, the Netherlands is fairly dark. The Dutch love to light candles and decorate their houses with them. One candle can change a lot of darkness. We each can light the way for others.

---

[14] J. Mandryk, *Operation World*, 624.

As a church, we are also trying to be lights for Jesus. We are conscious of initiating Christian outreach at this time of year in our church. We have hosted special services to make the light of Jesus Christ known to others. Many of these services target new people who may be interested in something about Christmas and the baby Jesus.

As a family we do one other activity that often lights the way for others to find Jesus. As many families in the Netherlands, we give gifts to each other, but then we also take time to give a gift to Jesus. So when we distribute the gifts around our family at Christmas, there is a time when we each share what gift we will give to Jesus. Many of these gifts over the years have served to light the way for others.

John's Gospel does not tell us the specific details of Jesus' birth. It does tell us overarching themes about the birth. It does so in terms of light and darkness and can guide our thinking about sharing the light of Jesus with others. John 1:5-10 reads as follows:

> The light shines in the darkness, but the darkness has not understood it. There came a man who was sent from God; his name was John. He came as a witness to testify concerning that light, so that through him all men might believe. He himself was not the light; he came only as a witness to the light. The true light that gives light to every man was coming into the world. He was in the world, and though the world was made through him, the world did not recognize him.

Darkness can be overcome when we light the way for others. May you bear witness to the light to those who need to know Jesus this Christmas!

*A prayer request for the Netherlands:*

With dwindling church attendance in the Netherlands, please pray for renewal and a new generation of Christian leaders to emerge in the Netherlands.

*Margré Hays*

# December 12:

# Albania – The Great

# Calling of God

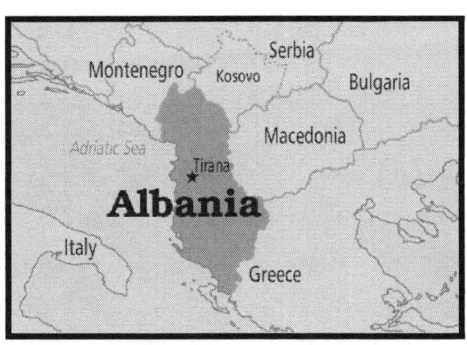

Albania is in the southeastern part of the European continent.
Adjacent to the Adriatic Sea, it is next to Greece, Serbia, and
Montenegro. We are a small country with just over 3 million
people.

While there were many Communist countries
surrounding us during the time of the Cold War, we were
unique. We were the only one to declare publicly our country
to be atheist. We did so in 1971 under our leader Enver
Hoxha. He told us that Islam had been the religion of the
Turkish occupier. Orthodoxy was the religion of the Greeks,
and Catholicism was the religion of Italian invaders and
Austrian imperialism. It was better just to be Albanian, which
he meant to be without any religion.

He did many other things in our country. Besides
declaring our nation to be atheist, he closed our borders. As a
result of his policies, my country became very isolated from
other nations. Nobody could enter or leave.

My father saw the effects of Enver Hoxha's reign on the
Christian community. He witnessed many attacks on the
church. For example, as a ten year old, he witnessed the
destruction of a Catholic Church in the city of Laç. The local

Communist party leader led a group of 200-300 people armed with sledgehammers to demolish the large Church there. The leader whipped people into a frenzy, invoking nationalistic feelings leading to the destruction of the building. My father heard stories from this time that some in the crowd were scared. Others felt that the icons within the Church were even shedding tears. It was a sad memory for him.

My father served as a captain in the Albanian army. His responsibility was to protect the borders of Albania. His specific charge was to listen for broadcasts indicating an American invasion.

While on duty listening to radio communications, my father came to know Jesus Christ as Savior and Lord. Instead of paying attention to possible American messages about an invasion of Albania, he decided to listen to a radio broadcast from Trans World Radio. This organization transmits the Christian message by radio into countries where it might otherwise not be heard.[15] The broadcast to which he was listening came from Monaco, a small country near Italy.

His decision to listen to this broadcast instead of doing his military duty could have put our family in great danger. If my father had been caught listening to the Trans World Radio message, he could have been thrown into prison or he could have lost his life. He was not caught, however, and after listening to several broadcasts, he eventually put his faith and trust in Jesus Christ. This changed our entire family's life and also the Christian community.[16]

---

[15] For further information about Trans World Radio, see website: http://www.twr.org.

[16] For this story see J. Butterworth, *God's Secret Listener: The Albanian Army Captain who Risked Everything* (Oxford/Grand Rapids: Monarch, 2010).

During the reign of Enver Hoxha, we could not celebrate Christmas publicly. The government wanted all celebrations to be on the New Year. For example, we did not have Christmas trees. Instead, they were called New Year's trees.

People were encouraged to gather with their families at New Year and have a family meal. The government even doubled the meat ration for that week. Christians, however, still celebrated Christmas. We did so secretly with a family meal.

Now that Communist times are over, Christmas is a time of great celebration in the church in Albania. On December 24 our entire church gathers for feasting, music, and dancing. The following morning we have a worship service. In the afternoon on Christmas Day, there is time to spend with family.

For me the joy on Christmas Eve and Christmas Day that is found within our church is especially meaningful. The unique thing about Christmas Eve and Christmas Day in our church is that everyone participates in one way or another. Some bring food, others decorate, others take part in clean up, and some will even wear costumes of the original Christmas participants – shepherds, wise men, etc.

I enjoy the shepherds in the Christmas story the most. They were called by God to come worship Jesus. Luke 2:8-11 tells us in the following verses.

And there were shepherds living out in the fields nearby, keeping watch over their flocks at night. An angel of the Lord appeared to them, and the glory of the Lord shone around them, and they were terrified. But the angel said to them, "Do not be afraid. I bring you good news of great joy that will be for all the people. Today in the town of David a Savior has been born to you; he is Christ the Lord."

God called the shepherds years ago. They brought their sheep and lambs to Jesus, and it reminds me of how the small and humble person can come and know Jesus. When God acts and calls his people, they will come, no matter what man may say. For years our country refused God, but his call is stronger still!

*A prayer request for Albania:*

The ban on the Christian religion was lifted in 1990. While the church has grown dramatically since then, there are still many towns and villages without a Christian presence. In some places where the Christian message has spread, there are spiritual lapses. Pray for the good news to continue to spread.

*Alta Mene*

# December 13:

# The Republic of

# Singapore – Creative

# Evangelism

The Republic of Singapore is a city state that is located off of the Malaysian peninsula in Southeast Asia. It is south of Thailand and Malaysia. It is north of Indonesia and only 137 kilometers (85 miles) from the equator. Singapore is a world class city with 3.7 million people, a large airport, and one of the busiest ports in the world.

It is also a diverse country. Our population is divided into at least 3 major ethnicities: Chinese, Malay, and Indian. There are also some Caucasians, too. My country also has a large percentage of immigrants. Just under half of the city population has been born from outside of our country.

Our diversity can be seen in the number of languages present within our small country which is only 272 square miles (or 704 square kilometers). Twenty-four languages are spoken, and we have four official languages. English is the primary language for education, and then there are three other official languages: Mandarin Chinese, Malay, and Tamil Indian. We are a multi-racial and multi-lingual society with freedom of religion.

At Christmas time, we are free to celebrate as we see fit. The challenge though in Singapore is with commercialism. This is overtaking the importance of Jesus' birth. For example, many throw a Christmas party whether one is a Christian or not. Many will throw parties in their homes and invite friends and relatives to come over for an evening of feasting. Many businesses will also celebrate the Christmas season in this way. They will throw Christmas parties for their employees and give gifts and cards to their clients. Some companies will also give all their employees half a day off on Christmas Eve. Many in Singapore just celebrate Christmas as a holiday with presents, parties, and feasting without reference to Jesus at all.

The churches are recognizing this and are now trying to use the Christmas season as a time for evangelism. In multi-ethnic Singapore we must be sensitive and culturally aware in our outreach. While there is freedom of religion, the government places limits on the public proclamation of religious beliefs. We had a number of bad experiences in the 1950s and 1960s when there were nationwide racial and religious riots. As a result, the government decrees that we cannot use words which could offend or poke fun at other religions. We cannot make one religion more superior than another either. We must be very careful as the government is careful about ensuring that religious harmony in the country is maintained.

Still, there are tactful ways to share the good news that Jesus has come. Many churches will host Christmas events with an evangelistic focus. It is fine to share the good news of Jesus following a Christmas play or a carol service when someone is in your church.

Many Christians will try individually to share with their friends about Jesus Christ, too. Some will invite carolers to come to a Christmas party to sing carols and share the good news that Jesus has come. The host will invite non-believing neighbors, relatives, friends, or colleagues to the party. Then, he will have these carolers come, sing, and share about the good news. My church in Singapore used to have an evangelistic caroling program which wove the gospel into and between the songs we sang. Imagine a mini-musical of traveling singers bringing the message to a captive audience (literally! They are all at the party, they can't leave lest be considered rude).

A Christmas carol that I particularly enjoyed from my years in Singapore is "A Thousand Candles." It is a carol about shining the light of Christ. The first lines go like this:

> We light a thousand candles bright
> Around the earth today
> And all the beams will shine across
> The heavens' grand display
> Yes over land and sea tonight
> The happy message brings
> The birth of Him our Lord and Christ
> Our Savior and our King.

Part of the Christmas story is about sharing that Jesus the light of the world has come. When the Gospel of John introduces Jesus, it introduces him as the light that is to go to everyone. We read of this in John 1:5-9 which says,

> The light shines in the darkness, but the darkness has not understood it. There came a man who was sent from God; his name was John. He came as a witness to testify concerning that light, so that through him all men might believe. He himself was not the light; he came only as a witness to the light. The true light that gives light to every man was coming into the world.

As you think of Christmas this year, let me encourage you to think of a way that you can shine the light. Even if you live in a place where you may need to be sensitive, there are still many creative ways to share the good news that Jesus Christ has come to earth.

*A prayer request for Singapore:*

Pray for Christians in Singapore as they share the good news of Jesus Christ this Christmas. Ask God to give them tact and sensitivity as they share that the light of the world has come.

*Hsiang-Ling Wee*

# December 14:

# Lithuania – Jesus of

# the Apostles

Lithuania is a country of approximately 3.5 million people along the Baltic Sea, north of Poland and Belarus, and near Russia. It is one of the three Baltic States along with the countries of Latvia and Estonia. We served for five years planting a church with the Church of England in the city of Klaipeda, Lithuania. It is a small city of approximately 180,000 people and is Lithuania's only seaport.

We celebrate Christmas on December 25, and it is nearly the coldest and darkest time of our year. Temperatures at this time of year range between 36 and 27 Fahrenheit (2 to -2 Celsius). The ground is often covered with snow, and most of the rivers and lakes are frozen. Portions of the Baltic Sea have frozen over. Pieces of ice float along in the Sea. Lithuania is also quite far north. As a result, Christmas time is a dark time of the year, too, with the sun rising at about 8 am and setting by about 3 pm. In the darkness and the cold, Lithuanians celebrate Christmas.

The bleak outdoor conditions are in stark contrast to the beautiful and symbolic Lithuanian Christmas tradition. As Christmas approaches, many Lithuanians fast, contemplate, and pray. Christmas Eve particularly is a day of strict fasting. People refrain from eating until they see the first star in the sky. During this time, people also prepare their homes. All linens and towels are washed in preparation of Christmas. They clean and tidy their homes in anticipation of Christmas Day.

Christmas Eve supper is the most important event in Christmas celebration for Lithuanian families. The table is set with a white linen table cloth. Underneath the table cloth, hay is strewn. This is a reminder as to how the baby Jesus was born. In the middle of the table is a crucifix along with a plate of *plotkeles* which are special Christmas wafers. The family sits around the table according to age. The oldest sits at the table head, while the youngest at the other end. Some homes leave a seat vacant, which is symbolic for Christ's presence.

The meal begins when the evening star appears in the sky. The meal starts with a prayer of thanksgiving for past blessings and a petition that the family remains intact during the coming year. The head of the house then breaks and shares the *plotkeles* with each member of the family, and they, in turn, with each other. Everyone wishes each other health and prosperity for Christmas and the New Year.

There are no less than 12 dishes served. Each of these dishes is without meat. Traditional dishes include: salty herring, prunes, dried peas, bread, whiting fish, boiled potatoes, sauerkraut, sweet wine, red beet soup, pastries with mushrooms, and oatmeal pudding. The twelve dishes are in honor of the twelve disciples.

The table setting reminds Lithuanians that Jesus Christ came as a baby in humility, being born in a stable, but then he went on to select the twelve disciples who became the apostles and the foundation of the Christian church (with the exception of Judas and the addition of Paul). He then offered his life upon a cross, providing salvation for all who will trust in his name. His presence is still with us today.

Does your Christmas have room for a Jesus who calls people to be part of a family built upon Jesus the Christ and then the foundation of the apostles? Lithuanian customs remind us that he not only came in a manger of hay, but that he also came to create God's household. He came to call disciples, give his life for us, and lead his people to holy living. His presence is with us today. It is a rich tradition in a harsh winter, which our world is like spiritually.

While not necessarily a Bible text that we read at Christmas time, Ephesians 2:19-22 does tell us of the great results of Jesus' life. It reads,

> Consequently, you are no longer foreigners and aliens, but fellow citizens with God's people and members of God's household, built on the foundation of the apostles and prophets, with Christ Jesus himself as the chief cornerstone. In him the whole building is joined together and rises to become a holy temple in the Lord. And in him you too are being built together to become a dwelling in which God lives by his Spirit.

May you realize in greater ways this Christmas that you, too, are a part of God's family built on Jesus, the cornerstone, and the apostles.

*A prayer request for Lithuania:*

Now that Communism no longer dominates Lithuania, new churches are growing rapidly within the country. Pray for good Christian teaching for the church that is based upon Jesus Christ and the teaching of the apostles.

*Roy & Joke Ball*

# December 15:

## The Philippines –

## Celebration amongst the

## Poor

Just south and east of China in the Pacific Ocean is my home country, the Philippines. It is an archipelago of over 7,000 islands with about 92 million people. It is the twelfth most populated country in the world. The city of Manila is the capital of our country and has about 1.5 million people in the space of only 38.55 kilometers (14.88 square miles). This makes Manila one of the most densely populated cities in the entire world.

If you have ever been to Manila, you will know that it is very busy. There is lots of traffic, the streets are crowded, and the city is overpopulated. There is a mixture of rich and poor people with a very large gap between them economically. On the one hand, there are many shopping malls which have the latest fashion from Hong Kong and Paris. On the other hand, there are also many slum areas, some of which are even built upon rubbish dumps.

Some reports say that 11 million people are living in what is known as Metro Manila, which encompasses 16 cities. The World Health Organization believes that approximately 2.2 million are living below the poverty line.[17] Many who live in the slums lack adequate water, housing, sanitation,

---

[17] World Health Organization, "Urgent steps must be taken to make Metro Manila healthier," World Health Organization,

education, health, and employment. People sleep in boxes at night.

In the center of Manila is a notorious rubbish dump called Smokey Mountain.[18] It is about 20 meters in height (65 feet), has over 2 million tons of waste, and has been a dumping place for Manila for 40 years. It is called Smokey Mountain because at times the heat from Manila will cause garbage to catch on fire. Some have even died in these fires.

It was closed in 1995, but an estimated 30,000 people still live near the landfill. Some are on top of the mountain under plastic and wooden sheeting. On Smokey Mountain dogs with rabies roam, chickens scratch in the rubbish, and children covered in dirt seek for empty plastic bottles and scraps of metal or paper. Many still make their life existence by foraging for scraps of recyclable material amongst the heap. They fill their sacks with these leftovers and then can receive a few cents so that they can live.[19]

In Manila, despite the economic divide, both poor and rich celebrate Christmas. Our Savior's birth shows no divide. In fact, some who are the most poor celebrate the greatest. Many begin planning for Christmas from September. People will start decorating from that month and keep decorations up through early January.

---

http://www.wpro.who.int/media_centre/press_releases/pr20100704.htm (Accessed March 7, 2011).

[18] Asian Development Bank, "Smokey Mountain Remediation Project: Summary of the Technical Report on Leachite Analysis, 1993 and 2006," http://www.adb.org/Projects/PEP/phi-smokey.asp (Accessed: December 5, 2010).

[19] Anna Coren, "Scratching out a Life on Manila's Smokey Mountain," http://edition.cnn.com/2010/WORLD/asiapcf/04/05/philippines.smokey.mountain/index.html (Accessed: December 5, 2010).

Christmas Eve is a very festive evening. This is a night for family gatherings and gift exchanges. We also shoot off fireworks. People are out in the streets, enjoying the celebration. Many do not know why they are celebrating, yet it is a fun time.

With all of the emphasis on celebration, it is important for our family to focus on the actual Christmas story. We read the Christmas story from the Bible. If we are a part of a large family gathering, we will have the whole family act out the story. We remember the poor, but we especially remember our Savior's birth.

Luke 2:6-7 says,

> While they were there, the time came for the baby to be born, and she gave birth to her firstborn, a son. She wrapped him in cloths and placed him in a manger, because there was no room for them in the inn.

Jesus came quietly being born in a stable. While he was rightfully the ruler and owner of this world, he was born in poverty. May you remember the poor this Christmas amidst your celebration!

*A prayer request for the Philippines:*

Pray for the poor in Manila. Over 5,000 people migrate to Manila daily and most start in the slums. Pray that God's love would reach them this Christmas. Ask God to bless ministries that work with the poor.

*Domingo Naz*

# December 16:

# Romania – Caroling after Communism

We are brothers from a family of seven and live in the town of Ştei. Our town has just over 8,000 people and is located in the northwestern corner of Romania. While most of the city is Romanian, we are not far from the country of Hungary and have some Hungarians amongst us as well as some gypsies.

We love to sing at Christmas. In the early evening on December 24, we have Christmas services at our church for a couple of hours. Afterwards, we go out singing in the city until close to midnight. Many from the church go through the streets of our town, processing with a large star before us. On the star is a picture of the nativity.

When the Communists ruled Romania, we were not able to do this. In fact, you could be arrested for singing Christmas carols publicly. Using the word "Christmas" or mentioning Christ or Mary could mean losing a job or being expelled from school. People treasured Christmas carols even during Communist times. They were never lost, and when Communism fell in 1989, we resumed this tradition of caroling in the streets on Christmas Eve.

People love to hear Christmas carols, and our church tries to visit as many homes in our town as possible. We sing carols that many would be familiar with in the West, such as "Joy to the World." Then, we sing a number of traditional Romanian Christmas carols such as *"Deschide uşa"*

("Christian Open Up Your Door"), "*O, ce veste minunată*" ("O How Wondrous News") and "*Trei păstori*" ("Three Shepherds"). When we sing, people respond by giving us candy, fruit, and nuts. Many will smile and share the joy that we have, too.

The lyrics of "*O, ce veste minunată*" ("O How Wondrous News") can be translated like this:

1. Oh, how wondrous news
Is shown to us from Bethlehem.
That the Pure Virgin
Has born a child
From the Holy Spirit.

2. As Joseph and Mary went
To Bethlehem, in order to be censed.
In a small shepherds' shelter,
Close to that town,
The Messiah was born.

3. Whom the Lord, who is before all ages,
Sent to us, so that He would come,
To be born,
To grow up,
And to save us all. [20]

Christmas caroling allows us to express our joy just as the angels did years ago. In Luke 2:10 we read, "And the angel said to them, 'Fear not, for behold, I bring you good news of a great joy that will be for all the people.'" Join with us in our joy this Christmas season!

---

[20] "Hymns and Carols of Christmas,"
http://www.hymnsandcarolsofchristmas.com/Hymns_and_Carols/oh_ho w_wondrous_news.htm (Accessed: March 24, 2010).

*A prayer request for Romania:*

The younger generation in Romania still suffers from the scars of Communism. Also, there are many orphans in Romania still. The HIV rate among them is the highest in Europe. Pray for all those who are working with these children that God would use them to love and reach out to this broken generation.

*Abel and Sam Coste*

# December 17:

## Republic of Armenia –

## Sovereignty at Christmas

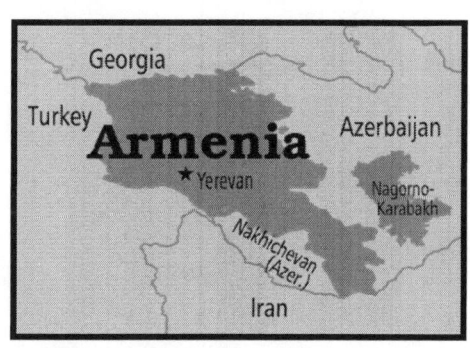

The Republic of Armenia is a landlocked country between Europe and Asia. We are located east of Turkey, west of Azerbaijan, north of Iran, and south of Georgia. At one time we were a former republic of the Soviet Union. Now, we are a modern republic.

Many do not know that Armenia was the first country officially to adopt the Christian faith. According to tradition, the Armenian Church was founded by Thaddeus and Bartholomew, two of Jesus' twelve apostles, who preached Christianity in Armenia in AD 40–60. Armenia declared itself a Christian country in approximately 301 A.D. Our country now recognizes the Armenian Apostolic Church as the national Church of our country. With such a history, there is a rich tradition of Christmas observance.

Christmas is not a one-day celebration as it is in many lands, but it is celebrated for many days, finally culminating on January 6. Christmas Day is entirely a Church holiday. For us, the Christmas service is what gives meaning to the Christmas holiday. Very few people gather in their homes to celebrate Christmas or give presents to their family members and friends.

There are many great traditions for Christians on Christmas Day. We greet each other in special ways at the Church. Here are a few Armenian Christmas greetings:

*Dzez yev mez medz avetis* (To you and us the good news)
*Qristos tsnav yev haytnvetsav* (Christ is born and revealed among us)
*Orhnyal e haydnootyun Qristosee* (Blessed is the revelation of Christ)

Traditionally, Armenian Christians fast during the week leading up to Christmas. Devout Armenians may even refrain from food for the three days leading up to Christmas Eve, in order to receive the Eucharist on a "pure" stomach. All the faithful, both young and old, fast. Many eat only one light meal a day on the week leading up to Christmas. The receiving of the Eucharist takes place on Christmas Eve (January 5), which is a service particularly rich in tradition.

On Christmas Eve, a special candlelight divine liturgy is celebrated in all Armenian Churches. Lighting candles symbolizes the light of the Star of Bethlehem leading the magi from the east to the baby Jesus. Following that evening service, people take candles that were lit in the Church to their homes. This symbolizes that the divine light and the blessing of the Church also extends to each home.

On Christmas Day, the Armenian Church has a unique divine liturgy, which is a special service of Holy Communion. It then also offers a Blessing of the Waters Service to celebrate the Baptism of Christ in the River Jordan. The Armenian Church then offers the special water to the faithful for spiritual and bodily healing.

When I reflect on the Christmas story, I am amazed at God's sovereignty displayed in the birth of Jesus. As I think about it, the question is not whether God would be able to accomplish what he had planned, but whether people would surrender their will to God's will. Neither Herod nor anyone on the earth could stop God from sending his Son, as Proverbs 21:30 says, "There is no wisdom, no insight, no plan that can succeed against the Lord." The wise men also could not miss finding him. Proverbs 8:17 says, "I love those who love me, and those who seek me find me."

God was and is always available and ready to bless those who seek him and are ready to obey his will. Neither the long distance, the danger of the journey, or Herod's threats could keep the wise men who were seeking Jesus from finding the Christ. That's what happens for true seekers. They always find their sovereign God.

May you respond to the greatness of our God this Christmas, and may you seek our Savior afresh and find him this holiday season!

*A prayer request for Armenia:*

A significant number of Armenians are a source of light to Christians in Russia and Muslim lands like Iraq and Iran. Pray that God would bless these faithful Armenians!

*Gegham Bdoyan*

# December 18: India Celebrating as a Community

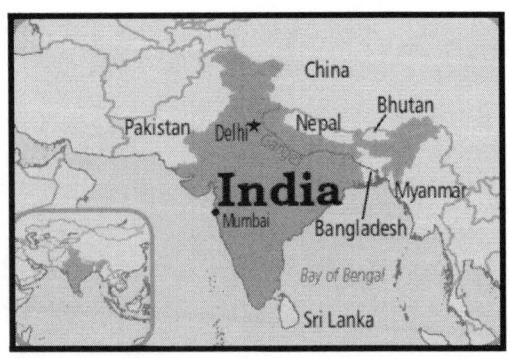

I come from the furthest eastern province in India, the province of Manipur. Our province is east of Bangladesh and west of Myanmar (formerly, Burma). The population of our region is over 2 million people. Imphal is the main city with just under 300,000 people.

While many people think of India as being only Hindu, there have been a variety of different religions in Manipur. Close to 60% of the people in Manipur are Hindu, and over 7% of the population are Muslim. There is also, however, a significant percentage of Christians. About 34% of the people in Manipur are Christian.

There was a time when Manipuris used to be animists. Animists worship spirits found in objects such as rocks, trees, rivers, and other such things. In Manipur people used to worship strong spirits, or the spirit which can inflict death. When many of our ancestors were animists years ago, they used to perform animal sacrifices as a part of their religious practices.

Hinduism entered the region in the fifteenth century. Hinduism has thousands of gods, and Hindus choose which ones they worship. Some of the more well-known gods in Hinduism are Vishnu, the creating god, Lakshmi, the goddess of beauty and wealth, Ganesh, the elephant-headed god of good fortune, and Shiva the destroying god. Hindus offer food, prayers, and money to these gods.

Into this religious context of animism and Hinduism, European missionaries came in the nineteenth century. They are responsible for the spread of Christianity in Manipur and especially in the hilly regions surrounding Manipur. While there was intense resistance at first, these missionaries persevered, leading many to Jesus Christ. They also initiated the spread of modern education among the tribal people.[21] Their sacrifice brought the good news of Jesus Christ to our land, and we now celebrate Christmas, too.

At Christmas time the many Christians in Manipur are in a joyful mood. The markets are filled with people buying and selling. It is common for Christians to buy new clothes since this is such a festive day.

On Christmas Day the churches in Manipur are filled with people. Many who do not attend church on other days attend church on this day for worship. Christians prepare for this time of year well in advance. Youth groups practice songs in preparation for Christmas services. We have a number of choirs that sing in these services.

---

[21] For further information on Christian mission in Manipur, India see Kh Menjor Singh, *History of the Christian Missions in Manipur and the Surrounding States* (New Delhi: Mittal, 1991).

Our church program starts on Christmas Eve, December 24. The program lasts all the way until December 26. Our Christmas services consist of prayers, readings from the Gospels, singing of hymns, and then sermons about Jesus Christ. After the church service we gather in an auditorium to sing. We gather to sing many songs that are familiar to those from the West also.

We also have a common dinner as a church on Christmas Day. We call it a *big feast* and we eat it outside in an open field with the whole church. We kill an ox, called a *mithun*, and roast it. The whole church will eat this ox, which we season with curry, along with additional food which we bring for this feast. After eating together, each returns home, but then we all return in the evening to worship.

Christmas for us is a celebration of our Savior's birth but also of the community that Jesus Christ has created. It is not my celebration or my family's experience alone. It is a joyful celebration that Jesus has come to earth to redeem his people.

Isaiah 9:2-3 foretells the joy that will come upon God's people at Jesus' birth. It says,

> The people walking in darkness have seen a great light; on those living in the land of the shadow of death a light has dawned. You have enlarged the nation and increased their joy; they rejoice before you as people rejoice at the harvest, as men rejoice when dividing the plunder.

We celebrate joyfully as a community. May you enjoy time with your church this Christmas, and may you find joy in your community celebration.

*A prayer request for India:*

There are many Christians in east India, but there is division between ethnic groups in Manipur. The divisions hamper outreach. Pray for reconciliation, ethnic harmony, and humility amongst the Naga, Kuki, and Paite people so that more in Manipur may know the joy that Jesus Christ has come.

*Muan Guite*

# December 19:

# Ghana – Leaving all to meet Jesus

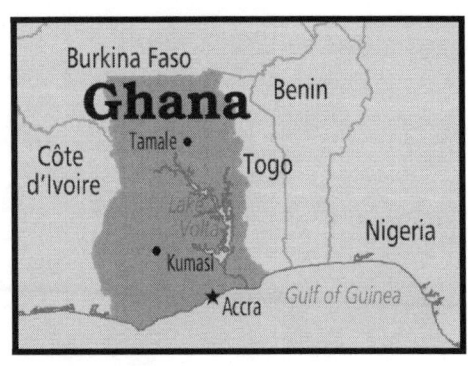

My home is in Tema, Ghana in West Africa. Tema is along the Atlantic Ocean and is the closest city to zero degrees latitude and zero degrees longitude. My city was once a small fishing town. In 1961 we built and opened the largest man-made harbor in all of Africa. With the construction of the harbor, the city grew greatly in size. It is now the largest harbor in the country of Ghana with over 200,000 people. Tema also has a sizeable oil refinery and an important manufacturing center.

While there is no snow or cold temperature since we are so close to the equator, we do love to celebrate Christmas. In fact, Christmas is the most important day of the year. On the night of December 24 people do not sleep due to the excitement in the air. On December 25 many people go to church in the morning. People visit their friends throughout the day, and some don costumes to walk through the streets on the way. Many come to visit my family since I am the pastor of a Pentecostal church in the city.

We celebrate by cooking a lot of food. We eat rice, chicken, and a dish that I particularly love called fufu. Many Africans love this dish. The fufu that we have is a thick and pasty red soup which is made from boiled goat's meat along with potatoes, cassava, and yams.

One aspect of the Christmas story that particularly challenges me is the visit of the wise men to Jesus. The wise men were very important people who traveled a long distance bringing expensive gifts. Even as a small child, I understood these men recognized the huge potential and respect that Jesus deserved.

Do you remember the way that they reacted to Jesus? We read about this in Matthew 2:11 which says,

> On coming to the house, they saw the child with his mother Mary, and they bowed down and worshiped him. Then they opened their treasures and presented him with gifts of gold and of incense and of myrrh.

Their visit to Jesus makes me think of my commitment and offering to Jesus. Would I be like the wise men at Jesus' birth? Would I have left a place of honor to go and search for Jesus? Would I have traveled so far and for such a long time? Would I give lavish gifts to Jesus? What about you?

*A prayer request for Ghana:*

Islam is growing across Ghana and conflicts and violence between Muslims and Christians are on the increase. Pray for the city of Tema, Ghana where many are turning to Islam. Pray for successful Christian outreach.

*Samuel Abeka*

# December 20:

# The Netherlands –

# Engaging Culture like Jesus

How can Christians rejoice and reach out at Christmas time in a region of the world where church attendance is falling and secularism is rising? We are actively considering this question at my Church in Rotterdam, the Netherlands. The city of Rotterdam where my family lives is the second largest city in the Netherlands with over 600,000 inhabitants. When the greater Rotterdam area is considered, the population is about 1 million people.

Besides the large population, there are many things that make Rotterdam an exciting city. Rotterdam has the largest harbor in Europe and welcomes shipping from around the world. The city is also filled with many modern buildings which replace the old architecture that was destroyed during the Second World War. New structures adorn the city such as Kijk-kubus, which are cubical houses. There is also the Erasmus Bridge, one of the longest cable bridges in Western Europe. This 800 meter bridge (approximately 2500 feet) crosses over the Maas River which runs through the city. You can see much of the city from the Euromast , a structure which reaches 100 meters (approximately 325 feet) into the air. Rotterdam is truly a thriving and modern city.

Many from outside of the Netherlands dwell in Rotterdam. Immigrant populations are also growing throughout the country. Of the 16.4 million inhabitants in the Netherlands, 3.2 million are first or second generation immigrants. Migrant communities are increasing in number and may comprise 17% of the population by the year 2015 and speak over 140 languages.[22] The immigrant population is especially noticeable in Rotterdam. The major groups of migrants who have settled down in Rotterdam include Turks, Surinamers, Cape Verdians, Moroccans, and Antillians, but there are many others.

There is a great need for the church to reach out to these migrant communities. These are especially open to hearing the good news of Jesus Christ in Rotterdam as well as in many places in Europe.[23] We need to reach out to this important group of people.

I serve as pastor of the Scots International Church, which by its name reveals its multi-national composition. The Church was established in 1643 to serve Scottish immigrants who had settled in Rotterdam. It has a long history of working with Scottish immigrants and now serves a multi-ethnic congregation. Beyond our normal Sunday morning worship, our Church building hosts a Portuguese congregation, an African congregation, a prayer service where prayers are offered in French, and meetings for pastors working with immigrants in Rotterdam.

---

[22] P. Johnston and J. Mandryk, *Operation World*, 475.
[23] P. Jenkins, *God's Continent: Christianity, Islam, and Europe's Religious Crisis* (New York: Oxford University Press, 2007), 55-102.

As a Church we are constantly trying to engage the culture critically.[24] We do not want to isolate ourselves, withdrawing from people. So while we are called the Scots International Church, we welcome all of our neighbors. At the same time, we do not want to become like the culture, mainstreaming ourselves and losing our Christian identity. While there are many different nationalities, there is only one way to God through Jesus Christ.

At Christmas time, we work to engage the culture. We invite the community to our Christmas services. We also take a Christmas carol service to the streets of Rotterdam. For several years we hosted a Christmas service in a park near our Church. It is held in the evening and by candlelight. As we open this community service, we give greetings in several languages. Different people from our Church will contribute to this outside service by reading poetry, singing, and even dancing. We also hold a life-size nativity play in the park. By taking Christmas to the streets, we hope to make the joy of our Savior accessible.

What ways can you critically engage your world this Christmas? Paul encourages Christians to welcome others in the Lord in Romans 15:7-9. It reads as follows:

> Therefore welcome one another as Christ has welcomed you, for the glory of God. For I tell you that Christ became a servant to the circumcised to show God's truthfulness, in order to confirm the promises given to the patriarchs, and in order that the Gentiles might glorify God for his mercy. As it is written, "Therefore I will praise you among the Gentiles, and sing to your name."

---

[24] For further information on this, consider my paper read at the Lausanne conference in South Africa. See website: http://conversation.lausanne.org/en/conversations/detail/10555.

Let me encourage you not to isolate yourself this Christmas or lose your identity in the surrounding culture. Years ago our Savior engaged the culture, too. He entered it, connected with it, but certainly did not lose his identity.

*A prayer request for the Netherlands:*

Pray for the many immigrants this Christmas in Western Europe. Ask God to use churches to reach out to this significant population with the good news of Jesus Christ.

*Robert Calvert*

# December 21:

## Republic of Cameroon –

## Like the Shepherds

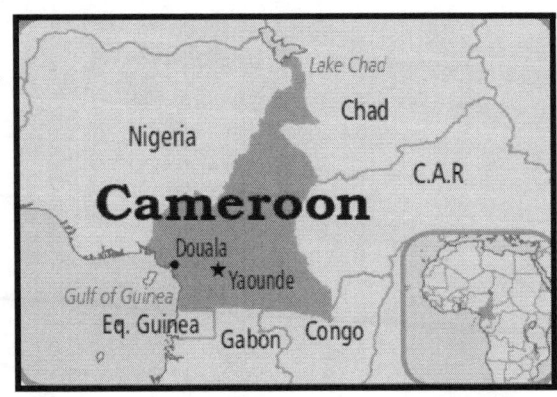

The Republic of Cameroon is located in central and western Africa. Nigeria borders us to the west, the country of Chad is to the northeast, and the Central African Republic is to the east. The countries of Equatorial Guinea, Gabon, and the Republic of the Congo border us to the south. We also have a coastline on the Bight of Bonny, which is part of the Gulf of Guinea and the Atlantic Ocean.

Like other countries in western Africa, God is doing a great work drawing people to his Son, Jesus Christ. In 1900, most in Cameroon would have been animists, worshiping different tribal deities. Now over fifty percent of our population is comprised of professing Christians.[25]

Christmas Day is an exciting one for Christians in my country. We celebrate by attending church services on Christmas Eve and Christmas Day. After church we hurry home to welcome and entertain extended family members and friends. We also visit the closest of our kindred and friends after attending to our own visitors.

---

[25] J. Mandryk, *Operation World*, 189.

The spirit of reconciliation reigns in our hearts at Christmas time.  Most Christmas messages in church emphasize love, humility, and reconciliation.  Pastors encourage their church members to love the unlovable, settle old scores, and reconcile with offenders in the family, the church, and the community.

As an African, I identify greatly with the poverty and suffering at the first Christmas.  Many in my country are living in poverty.  While Cameroon's economy is stronger than other nations in Africa, our standard of living is much lower than many Western nations.  Cameroon is a "low-income and food-insecure country" according to the World Food Program, a United Nations organization which fights hunger worldwide.  In Cameroon 40.2 percent of our 19 million people live below the poverty line which is one US dollar per day.  If one goes to the rural areas, 52.1 percent live below the poverty line. [26]

I identify with the shepherds who also lived in poverty but were the first to receive the news of Jesus' birth.  The lifestyle of those shepherds reminds me of the toil of African life.  They were the rural, poor people with low social status, and they lived similar to that of most Cameroonians.  The poor and suffering shepherds were watching their flock by night, yet the heavenly minstrels chose to announce the birth of the Savior to them first.

It is my custom to celebrate Christmas in the rural communities.  As part of the celebration, we sing a Christmas carol called "Still the Night."  When I hear this carol and see hills with sheep and shepherds all around me, then the Christmas story comes to life. The lowly birth of Christ and

---

[26] World Food Program, "Cameroon," World Food Program, http://www.wfp.org/countries/cameroon (Accessed:  May 23, 2011).

then his exaltation as king allows the poor (and also the rich) to identify with the Savior at Christmas.

Here is one verse from this song:

Still the night, Holy the night,
Shepherds first saw the light,
Heard resounding clear and strong,
Far and near, the Angels' song,
Christ the Redeemer is here,
Christ the Redeemer is here.

There is one Scripture text that touches me at Christmas time in particular. Isaiah 53:2-3 prophesies of the poverty that Jesus would experience and reads as follows:

He grew up before him like a tender shoot, and like a root out of dry ground. He had no beauty or majesty to attract us to him, nothing in his appearance that we should desire him. He was despised and rejected by men, a man of sorrows, and familiar with suffering. Like one from whom men hide their faces he was despised, and we esteemed him not.

Although rich in glory, he was born meek and lowly in a manger.

As a Christian believer, I am also challenged that God calls me to be humble in some circumstances. There may be times that he expects me to give up my social status, and self-importance for his sake and for the sake of serving the poor. Jesus denied his heavenly glory, his social status, and satisfaction in order that he may change my spiritual status from sinner to saint. I hope that you will think of identifying with the lowly and being increasingly humble this Christmas, too.

*A prayer request for Cameroon:*

Pray for those in poverty this Christmas.  Ask God to meet their physical needs but also to find Jesus Christ, the bread of life.  Pray that the church in Cameroon would effectively address both of these needs.

*Gideon Yungwa Nchinda*

# December 22:
## Democratic Socialist Republic of Sri Lanka –
## Peace amidst Fear

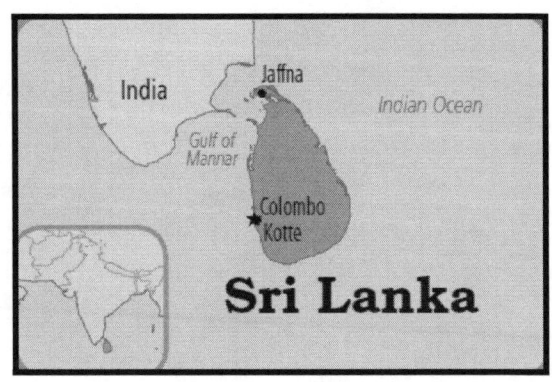

Off of the southeastern coast of India in the Indian Ocean is the Democratic Socialist Republic of Sri Lanka. Although our country is an island, we have over 20 million inhabitants. Colombo, the city where we are from, is the capital of Sri Lanka. It has the largest population of any city in Sri Lanka with over 600,000 inhabitants.

There are a variety of different religions on Sri Lanka -- Muslim, Hindu, and Christian. The majority of Sri Lanka is Buddhist, which is also the state religion. There is a long history of Buddhism that stretches back to the 2nd century BC in Sri Lanka.

Buddhists believe in reincarnation, and they believe that each person lives many lives. According to the Buddhist religion, everyone is supposed to do good deeds in this life. By doing these, he or she may be reborn to a higher standing in one's next life, perhaps becoming wealthy or famous. If someone does bad things, then he or she will be reborn into poverty or into a life of suffering. The goal of the Buddhist religion is to break the cycle of life and death. This happens when someone finally reaches the end of suffering and achieves *nirvana*.

Buddhists worship in temples. In our city of Colombo, there are several Buddhist temples. They are decorated ornately with gold statues, paintings, and bells. Each temple has a statue of Buddha. Worshippers come to these temples each day seeking merit. They burn incense in front of the Buddha. They also meditate, pray, and leave offerings such as candles or flowers. These acts are supposed to bring inner peace.

While many in Sri Lanka pursue peace by their Buddhist devotions, our country has been far from peaceful recently. Two groups of people – the Sinhalese (Buddhist) and the Tamil (Hindu) people have been fighting with each other. Some of the Tamil people believe that the largely Sinhalese government has treated them unfairly. In the northeastern part of Sri Lanka, the Tamil people have even been fighting to form a new state that would be Hindu. In this fierce conflict, children have been used unfairly as front line soldiers. Many people have lost relatives as a result of this fighting.

Buddhist extremists in our country have also persecuted Christians. They see the Christian faith as a foreign influence and a colonial imposition. These extremists want to limit foreign funding, inhibit the building of churches, and make conversions to Christianity "illegal." As a result, Buddhist extremists have burned many churches and homes.

Because the persecution has been so severe, a group that monitors Christian persecution named *Voice of the Martyrs* considers Sri Lanka to be a hostile nation.[27] For example, they

---

[27] Voice of the Martyrs, "Sri Lanka: Church Attacked," Voice of the Martyrs, http://www.persecution.com/public/restrictednations.aspx?clickfrom=b WFpbl9tZW51 (Accessed: March 20, 2011).

report that on November 5, 2009 about 200 members of the Buddhist-led political party Jathika Hela Urumaya attacked the Jesus Never Fails Good News Centre Church in Koswatta, Sri Lanka, which is east of Colombo. The attackers hurled stones at the building and threatened to kill the pastor, accusing him of unethical conversions.

Turmoil is not found in every place in Sri Lanka. Our family attends a church in Colombo, and this church is not experiencing persecution in our city. At Christmas time, we celebrate Christmas with nativity plays in the church. These plays are held in both the Sinhalese and Tamil languages. Many come from the community to view these plays. We will also take our joy outside of the church to others. We go caroling to people in our community as a church. We also raise money to give to charity. We feel safe to express our joy, but our church is very aware that others nearby in our country are afraid and are also suffering for the faith that we proclaim freely.

While many think of the first Christmas as a peaceful time, not everything was peaceful at the first Christmas either. We read of this in Matthew 2:3-8, 12 which reads as follows.

> When King Herod heard this he was disturbed, and all Jerusalem with him. When he had called together all the people's chief priests and teachers of the law, he asked them where the Christ was to be born. "In Bethlehem in Judea," they replied, "for this is what the prophet has written: "'But you, Bethlehem, in the land of Judah, are by no means least among the rulers of Judah; for out of you will come a ruler who will be the shepherd of my people Israel.'" Then Herod called the Magi secretly and found out from them the exact time the star had appeared. He sent them to Bethlehem and said, "Go and make a careful search for the child. As soon as you find him, report to me, so that I too may go and worship him." And having been warned in a dream not to go back to Herod, they returned to their country by another route.

Herod was fearful of the Christ child, thinking that he would overtake his reign.  The Magi experienced Herod's fear when they met him on the way to find Jesus.  We, too, as Sri Lankan Christians live with an awareness of fear but also with joy that Jesus has been born.  While there may be threats to Christians nearby, God's kingdom still advances as it did years ago.

*A prayer request for Sri Lanka:*

The violence of Buddhist extremists against Tamil Hindus and Christians has shattered the illusion that Buddhism is a religion of peace. Pray that in the uncertainty in the Democratic Socialist Republic of Sri Lanka, many would begin to look for Jesus.  Also pray for Christians in Sri Lanka to remain faithful during persecution.

*Druvi and Sandy Jayamanne*

# December 23:

# Hong Kong –

# The Supreme Gift

The city of Hong Kong is where I was raised. It is a densely populated city with approximately 7 million people. It is located on the south side of China and against the South China Sea.

It is also one of two special administrative districts within the People's Republic of China. When I was born, Hong Kong was a British colony. The British ruled over my city from 1842 which is the year Hong Kong was ceded to them at the end of the First Opium War (1839-1842). On July 1, 1997 Hong Kong was handed over peacefully to the People's Republic of China. It is now a special administrative region, and maintains its own autonomy except in defense and foreign affairs. So while Hong Kong is now a part of the People's Republic of China, it still retains a great amount of western influence.

You will be impressed by a number of things if you come to my city. Our architecture will get your attention. Hong Kong has the tallest skyline of any city with four of the twenty tallest buildings in the world. The tallest building in Hong Kong, called the International Commerce Center, is the fourth tallest building in the world with one hundred and eight stories. These big buildings can be found next to colonial era buildings which are more than one hundred and fifty years old. The contrast is striking.

You will also notice the frantic shopping districts. Buying and selling takes place from early in the morning until late in the evening. Hong Kong has long been the shopping capital of Asia. You can find anything that you want to buy in my city. There are high end boutiques to bargain basement markets.

At Christmas time, consumerism especially overtakes Hong Kong. Streets are filled with merchants, customers, decorations, lights, and advertisements. The Tsai Shat Sui Street is particularly famous in this regard. It is a winding street with many shops and is arrayed with lights and symbols of Christmas such as Santa Claus, shepherds, and the baby Jesus. People fill the shops on this street during Christmas, looking for the best gifts for their family.

Many Hong Kong families also flock to the big shopping malls. These malls try to outdo each other with the most imaginative and extravagant Christmas decorations. Times Square boasts the tallest Christmas tree, and Pacific Place is well loved by children for its mini playground, which has a different theme every Christmas season.

Shopping in Hong Kong is not only bright lights and advertisements. Unlike the West, merchants are very aggressive and engage shoppers in the streets, trying to entice customers to come into their stores and buy their merchandise. Some guides to Hong Kong even consider shopping anywhere from a "social activity" to a "serious sport."

There are common tricks that shop owners use. Many of them hand out small gifts to children who are accompanying their parents on shopping treks. This entices the children as well as their parents to come into the store. Sometimes merchants go into the streets and invite families to take pictures with Santa Claus. Afterwards, they will offer the family free child care. While the children are happy and taken care of, parents are then more free to shop in their stores.

Other shop owners bargain about prices in the streets. This can be quite animated with buyer and seller proposing different prices, arguing with each other, and at times walking away from each other in disgust. Sometimes a merchant will invite a customer to tea in his store. This "hospitality" serves to soften up the customer. A little later when the bargaining begins, the merchant will be seen to be a friend and the customer will be more likely to buy than to negotiate.

You might think that on Christmas Day that the stores will be closed, but they are open even then. The buying and consuming continues. It never seems to stop!

This is a great challenge for Christians in Hong Kong. Our church is not far from the shopping districts. Our families enter our church from the frantic shopping on the streets. We try as a church to help quiet people before and during the service. We also deliberately lead the service so that we will think about the meaning of Christ's birth. Jesus left heaven and came to be a Savior to all those who trust him. His birth is the true gift.

Galatians 4:4-7 speaks of the true gift at Christmas time. Paul writes,

> But when the time had fully come, God sent his Son, born of a woman, born under law, to redeem those under law, that we might receive the full rights of sons. Because you are sons, God sent the Spirit of his Son into our hearts, the Spirit who calls out, "Abba, Father." So you are no longer a slave, but a son; and since you are a son, God has made you also an heir.

Jesus came to redeem us from slavery to sin and make us his sons. This is the supreme gift. Let me encourage you this Christmas to focus on the true gift. Don't let Christmas shopping divert you from what the true gift is this Christmas!

*A prayer request for Hong Kong:*

Pray for the church in Hong Kong. Ask God to keep the increasing wealth and materialism from draining Christian commitment.

*Sau Ping Louie*

# December 24:

# Republic of

# Kazakhstan –

# God with Us

In Central Asia, south of Russia, west of China, and north of Uzbekistan, Kyrgyzstan, and Turkmenistan is the Republic of Kazakhstan. It was formerly a Soviet Republic until it declared its independence in 1991. It is the ninth largest country in the world. Almaty is in the far southeast of the country and is a large city of over 1.3 million people.

The people in Almaty are quite diverse. Over half are Kazakh people who are descendants from Turkish people. Many of them can trace their ancestry to nomadic tribes that roamed the steppes of modern-day Kazakhstan. Russians are the second largest group of people in our city, and then there are Uighur and Tatar people.

Now that the Republic of Kazakhstan is not under Communist rule, it has religious freedom. Most were atheists during the Communist era. The largest religious belief in this country is Islam, but then there are also a number of Christians. Some Muslims are devout, but many are not. Some professing Muslims are merely trying to connect with religious beliefs from their ancestry.

With Kazakhstan's history as a former Soviet Republic coupled with Islam's influence, celebrating Jesus' birth is a relatively new event. On December 25, people go to work, and it is a normal school day for children. A small number of people may celebrate Christmas on January 7, but most have never celebrated Jesus' birth.

As church planters we decided to introduce the celebration of Jesus' birth into the church with which we work. We could have left the event out of our church life, but we felt that it would help those who attend to understand the overall plan that God is accomplishing throughout history.

We often have a Christmas pageant for the children. The children dress up as Mary, Joseph, wise men, angels, and shepherds. This helps to let them know about the Christmas story from an early age.

Catherine has led a women's group with an Advent Calendar and the Jesse tree. This is a tree that is decorated each week with ornaments or objects that represent Old Testament events from Creation to the Birth of Jesus. The ornaments are handmade and added each day leading up to Christmas. There is also a verse of Scripture related to the Christmas story represented with each ornament. By using the Jesse tree, it shows how Jesus' coming to earth was a part of God's great plan.

On Christmas Eve our church holds a candlelight service. We often use the theme of light and darkness in the service and then share that Jesus is the true light, spoken of ages ago, who came to bring light to the nations and be with us. We always close the service with the singing of

"Immanuel, Our God is with us" by Michael Card. This song also provides a great picture of God's plan throughout history. The song is based on the Old Testament passage of Isaiah 7:14 in which Jesus is first called Immanuel, which means God with us. The passage reads, "Therefore the Lord himself will give you a sign: The virgin will be with child and will give birth to a son, and will call him Immanuel."

The lyrics of this song go like this:

Immanuel, Immanuel, His name is called, Immanuel.
God with us, Who has forgiven us,
His name is called, Immanuel.

May God's overall plan throughout history inspire you this Christmas season as it is inspiring young believers in the Republic of Kazakhstan!

*A prayer request for Kazakhstan:*

The church in Kazakhstan is alive and becoming strong. The church is especially growing among young people. Pray that this numerical growth may continue and also that the church may mature accordingly.

*Dan & Catherine Burns*

# December 25:
# Federal Republic of
# Nigeria –Savoring
# the Moment

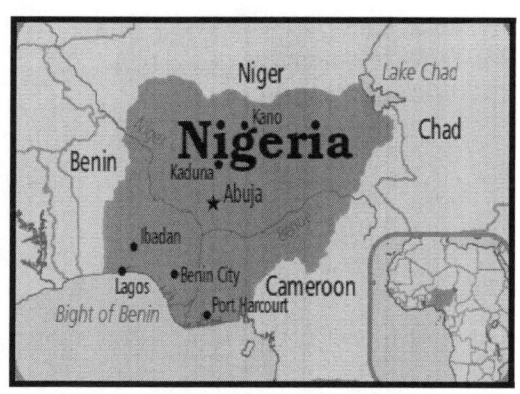

If you are looking for a white Christmas, you will not find it in my homeland. If you are looking for a place where there are many joyful Christians, however, you will find it in Nigeria. My country is located just north of the equator in Africa, near the countries of Cameroon, Chad, Benin, and Niger in West Africa. We are the most populous country in Africa, and we know how to celebrate Christmas.

Christmas is a relatively new celebration for us because for many years Christianity was not a part of our country. Before the sixteenth century, Nigerians had mostly tribal ethnic religions. We worshiped gods in rocks and trees, and others worshiped their ancestors. Some also worshiped spirits, oracles, magic, and mystical agents. In the northern part of Nigeria, Islam had made inroads, too, but not Christianity.

The Christian faith came to my country in the 1500s as a result of missionaries from Europe. The Christian church has grown dramatically since then, particularly in the last 100 years.

Now in 2010, nearly 81 million people claim the Christian faith. Some thus see 48% of the population as Christian,[28] while others about 51%.[29]   In either case, what a great transformation has taken place in our country over the past 500 years!

Christmas is an important day for us in Nigeria. Many prepare for this day well in advance of December. Many make plans to travel and see friends and family. It is a time that many return home to spend a few weeks with relatives.

As you get closer to December, different groups of people will make plans for celebrating Christmas. Groups of 5 to 10 people will contribute money towards buying meat for a large Christmas meal. Families will make preparations for extra food so that they can share with those without enough food. Not everyone has enough to eat in Nigeria. Sharing food at Christmas is important. Not to share would be unloving.

Church life becomes very festive as Christmas Eve draws close. Members will practice songs to be sung at the Christmas Eve service. Others rehearse plays that depict Jesus' birth. On Christmas Eve we gather as a church for a 2-3 hour service. At this service, several pastors will preach messages about the birth of Jesus. We also will sing many Christmas carols.

My favorite carol is "While Shepherds Watched their Flocks by Night." While it was written in the early 18th century by an Irishman far away from my country, the carol

---

[28] BBC, "Nigeria: Facts and Figures," BBC News
http://news.bbc.co.uk/2/hi/africa/6508055.stm (Accessed: May 14, 2011).
[29] Operation World, "Nigeria," Operation World,
http://www.operationworld.org/nigr (Accessed: December 7, 2010).

gives us a good picture of what happened at Jesus' birth. This carol helps me to picture the first Christmas in my mind. With all the other festivities happening, it is important for me to savor that great event of many years ago.

The lyrics of this great carol are from Luke 2:8-14 and are as follows:

While shepherds watched their flocks by night,
All seated on the ground,
The angel of the Lord came down,
And glory shone around,
And glory shone around.

"Fear not!" said he, for mighty dread
Had seized their troubled mind.
"Glad tidings of great joy I bring
To you and all mankind
To you and all mankind."

"To you, in David's town, this day
Is born of David's line
A Savior, who is Christ the Lord,
And this shall be the sign,
And this shall be the sign."

"The heavenly Babe you there shall find
To human view displayed,
All meanly wrapped in swathing bands,
And in a manger laid,
And in a manger laid."

Thus spake the seraph and forthwith
Appeared a shining throng
Of angels praising God on high,
Who thus addressed their song,
Who thus addressed their song:

"All glory be to God on high,
And to the Earth be peace;
Good will henceforth from Heaven to men
Begin and never cease,
Begin and never cease!"

Celebrating Christmas Day has no national or historical boundaries. The Christmas story and the great carols are loved worldwide. May you celebrate Christmas day with intense joy as the shepherds did years ago and as we do in Nigeria now!

*A prayer request for Nigeria:*

The church in Nigeria has grown quickly and rapidly. Pray that this growth in the Christian faith would be followed by good teaching that will strengthen the church.

*Jonathan Kinchai*

# December 26: Spain – Only the Beginning

Our family served in Spain as missionaries for twenty years. Spain is located in the southwest corner of Europe. It has historically been a Roman Catholic country. Recently there has been a growing secularism.

According to a July 2009 study by the Spanish Center of Sociological Research, about 73% of Spaniards identify themselves as Catholics and 2% belong to other faiths. There are now about 22% who identify with no religion at all. Most Spaniards do not participate regularly in religious services. Of those Spaniards who identify themselves as religious, 58% hardly ever or never go to church, 17% go to church some times each year, 9% some times per month and 15% every Sunday or multiple times per week.[30]

During Christmas time some people will go to church to celebrate the birth of Jesus. Unfortunately, most never understand that Christmas is much more than an isolated event. I think we must see Christmas in connection with the whole sweep of biblical history.

---

[30] Spanish Center of Sociological Research, "Barometro de Julio," Centro de Investigaciones Sociológicas, http://www.cis.es/cis/opencms/-Archivos/Marginales/2800_2819/2811/es2811.pdf (Accessed: October 16, 2010).

I once gave a series of Advent messages in which I used Isaiah 53. I cannot exactly remember the title of the messages, but one of them was along the lines of "Jesus was born to die." Anything less (viewing the Nativity in isolation) is not worthy of God's great plan and work of redemption.

The first five verses of Isaiah 53 tell of this. They read:

> Who has believed our message and to whom has the arm of the LORD been revealed? He grew up before him like a tender shoot, and like a root out of dry ground. He had no beauty or majesty to attract us to him, nothing in his appearance that we should desire him. He was despised and rejected by men, a man of sorrows, and familiar with suffering. Like one from whom men hide their faces he was despised, and we esteemed him not. Surely he took up our infirmities and carried our sorrows, yet we considered him stricken by God, smitten by him, and afflicted. But he was pierced for our transgressions, he was crushed for our iniquities; the punishment that brought us peace was upon him, and by his wounds we are healed.

Jesus grew up like a root out of dry ground, which I believe to be a prophecy of the virgin birth. Then, he was despised and rejected, and suffered for us. It was part of God's plan that he would be despised and rejected for our benefit.

Later in Isaiah 53 we see the purpose of his rejection in verses 10-11.

> Yet it was the LORD's will to crush him and cause him to suffer, and though the LORD makes his life a guilt offering, he will see his offspring and prolong his days, and the will of the LORD will prosper in his hand. After the suffering of his soul, he will see the light *of life* and be satisfied; by his knowledge my righteous servant will justify many, and he will bear their iniquities.

Because of God's overall purpose, Jesus will not only be born, but suffer, see death, and be raised.  Many will be saved because this is God's plan that is far beyond his birth.  God has a great plan for the redemption of the world.  Christmas is only the beginning!

*A prayer request for Spain:*

There has not been the longed-for turning to a personal relationship to Christ as religious freedom has increased in Spain.  Pray that those who are embracing secularism will embrace Jesus.

*Ellis Brotzman*

# December 27:

# Myanmar – Be a Star

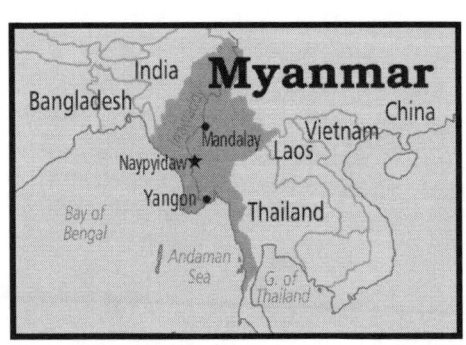

I come from the country of Myanmar, which was formerly known as Burma. Myanmar is the largest country geographically in southeast Asia. It borders China, Laos, Bangladesh, Thailand, and India.

I come from the northern part of the Chin state, which is in the northwest part of the country. It is a mountainous area with fewer transportation links with the rest of the country. The British ruled in the Chin State from 1885. American missionaries arrived in the 1890s and by the middle of the twentieth century, these missionaries had converted most of the Chin people to the Christian faith. A sizable minority, however, is either animistic or Buddhist.

We celebrate Christmas as a church but not as families. We will gather for a Christmas Eve Service on December 24 and then a service in the morning and the evening on December 25.

On Christmas Day, there is a Christmas gift exchange within the church. Different members will place gifts in the Christmas tree in the church. One by one each member will take a gift from the tree. Then, it will be another church member's turn. After this we all eat together as a church a meal consisting of pork, chicken, and rice.

While the Chin State of Myanmar is largely Christian, the rest of the country is predominantly Buddhist. There are over 37 million Buddhists in comparison to just fewer than 4 million Christians.

Buddhists in Myanmar believe that salvation comes from doing good works, meditation, or practices such as the recitation of spells, magic, or alchemy. By doing these deeds, Buddhists aim to escape the cycle of birth and rebirth, which they believe all human beings experience, and reach *nirvana*, a place where one is free from suffering forever.

Some Buddhists in Myanmar, especially those from the rural areas, have many superstitions. These include astrology, palmistry, and clairvoyance. Buddhists rely on these practices to make important decisions regarding marriage, business partnerships, naming a baby, etc. They also believe that certain good deeds can be performed to offset bad luck. Such deeds may include setting some live birds or animals free, building a footbridge, or mending a road.

While Buddhists believe in a spiritual realm, they do not believe in a God that rules the universe. They certainly do not believe that Jesus Christ is the Son of God who came to earth to free people from their sins.

Monasticism is also a practice amongst Buddhists in Myanmar. Monks wear full length red garments and shave their heads. They meditate and study a great deal, too. Our country has a large number of monks. They have even attempted to influence politics recently when they stood up to the military Junta in 2007.

Within this Buddhist context, Christmas is a time of evangelism for my church. As their preacher, I tell my church members, as the star guided people to find Jesus at Christmas long ago, they are now to be a star for others. We find that Buddhists are open to hearing about Jesus at Christmas time.

There is a Buddhist monk who recently moved into our village. He is attracting students to his school where he teaches Buddhism. We invited this monk and his students to eat with us at Christmas, and then we shared the good news with him. I believe that many Buddhists come to trust Jesus Christ as Savior and Lord during Christmas. To whom can you be a star this Christmas time?

Matthew 2:1-2 reads,

> After Jesus was born in Bethlehem in Judea, during the time of King Herod, Magi from the east came to Jerusalem and asked, "Where is the one who has been born king of the Jews? We saw his star in the east and have come to worship him."

*A prayer request for Myanmar:*

The military regime in Myanmar is seeking to isolate and marginalize the church. Please pray for the removal of restrictions on fellowship with Christians of other lands. Also pray for fortitude and faithfulness among believers amidst persecution.

*Cin Lian Mang*

# December 28:

# Ukraine –

# Faith Overcomes

Ukraine is a large country in East Europe. The Russian Federation borders my country to the north and the east. On our western border are Belarus, Poland, Slovakia, and Hungary. Romania and Moldova are southwest, and the Black Sea and the Sea of Azov are southeast of Ukraine. Ukraine was once a part of the former Soviet Union. In 1991 we declared independence from Russia, and now we are independent.

I am from the city of Zaporozhye, a city of over 750,000 people in the southeast corner of the Ukraine. My city of Zaporozhye is on the banks of the Dnieper River and a little less than 400 miles (about 600 kilometers) south and east of Kiev, the capital city.

I attend a Ukrainian Baptist Church that is 125 years old. Many may not know that the Baptist Church in Ukraine is one of the oldest and widespread Protestant denominations in our country. There are other Protestant denominations such as the Lutheran and Mennonite denominations, but the Baptists and Pentecostals are the largest Protestant denominations in Ukraine.

During Communist times, Ukrainian Baptists faced a lot of pressure. The Soviet regime tried to force everyone to adopt atheism. This was based on Karl Marx's belief that "religion was the opium of the people." The longer quote shows that religion must be abolished and reads like this:

> Religion is the sigh of the oppressed creature, the heart of a heartless world, and the soul of soulless conditions. It is the opium of the people. The abolition of religion as the illusory happiness of the people is the demand for their real happiness.[31]

The Communist leadership believed Marx and tried to stamp out Christianity in the Soviet Ukraine. They banned publication of Bibles, Christian books, and other religious materials. They also made it illegal to attend church, and they closed seminaries. Some churches were destroyed, and church property was confiscated for public use. From the 1920s, our church was illegal in Soviet Ukraine. Many Christians were sent to mental hospitals, labor camps, and prisons. Thousands died for their faith during Communist times.

While attempting to crush the church, the Soviet regime also actively promoted atheism. People in our country were taught atheism in the schools, through the media, and also through other organizations. The government formed groups to promote atheism. For example, in the 1920s through the 1940s, the League of the Militant Godless was formed to propagate atheism. This was a large volunteer organization composed of workers, students, and peasants and was supported by the Communist party. This group published anti-Christian material, ridiculed religion, and promoted atheism.

---

[31] See Karl Marx, *Early Writings* (New York: Vintage, 1975), 244.

Despite all of the opposition during Communist times, our denomination remained strong. Even during Communist times, the Soviet Ukraine had the most Baptist believers of any other nation in the world besides the United States.[32] In August 2009, we as Ukrainian Baptists celebrated our 400th anniversary. There are over 200,000 Ukrainian Baptists in Ukraine today.

We celebrate Christmas on 25 December, but the main day for the celebration of Christmas in Ukraine is January 7. This is the day when the Orthodox Church celebrates Christmas. On that day our church of over 500 people gathers to worship. We have many special guests, and some of them preach that day. Christmas Day services may have 3 or 4 sermons. There is also a lot of singing with likely 15 different songs in the service. Some of these are sung by trios, while others sing solos. A few hymns are sung by the whole congregation.

I have sung in the choir for a few years. I knew a lot of these songs in my youth, but when I finally gave my life to the Lord, suddenly these Christmas songs that I had known for many years took on a new meaning. One of the Christmas songs that we sing in the Ukraine can be translated in this way:

> Today the biggest joy has come that we ever had.
> This new star shines over Bethlehem; Jesus was born here.
> He became human, he was wrapped in swaddling clothes,
> So we sing praise to the Lord, we praise Christ.

---

[32] Catherine Wanner, "Evangelicalism and Resurgence of Religion in Ukraine," University Center for International Studies University of Pittsburgh, http://www.ucis.pitt.edu/nceeer/2006_819_19g_Wanner.pdf (Accessed: March 11, 2011).

Even though Communism oppressed us, the Christian faith endures. One Bible passage that speaks of the enduring nature of the Christian faith can be found in Romans 8:35-39. It reads as follows:

> Who shall separate us from the love of Christ? Shall trouble or hardship or persecution or famine or nakedness or danger or sword? As it is written: "For your sake we face death all day long; we are considered as sheep to be slaughtered." No, in all these things we are more than conquerors through him who loved us. For I am convinced that neither death nor life, neither angels nor demons, neither the present nor the future, nor any powers, neither height nor depth, nor anything else in all creation, will be able to separate us from the love of God that is in Christ Jesus our Lord.

How wonderful it is to celebrate Christmas in a land where persecution has ended. There is nothing that can overcome the love of God as seen in Jesus Christ his only son.

*A prayer request for Ukraine:*

The Ukrainian church experienced intimidation and manipulation during the Communist years. While the church has emerged stronger from that time, pray that freedom of religion will be truly felt and experienced within Ukraine.

*Olga Zykova*

# December 29:

# Ethiopia –

# Suffering for Me

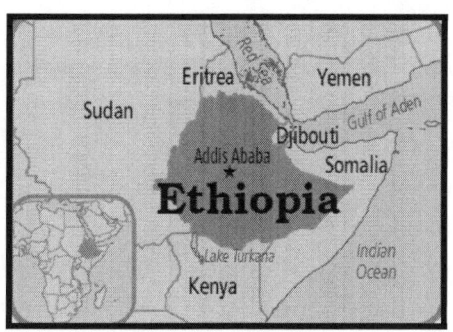

My family is from the country of Ethiopia in East Africa. Our country is on the horn of Africa, a peninsula which juts out into the Arabian Sea. Ethiopia is south of Eritrea, north of Kenya, east of Sudan, west of Djibouti and Somalia. It is the second most populated country in Africa with approximately 82 million people in it. My city of Addis Ababa has over 3 million inhabitants. It is the capital city of Ethiopia and also of the African Union.

You may be familiar with Ethiopia from the headlines in the news over the past number of years. Our country was in a war with neighboring Eritrea from 1998-2000. This came about due to disputed territories between our two countries. Tens of thousands died on both sides during this war. There are still threats that this conflict will resume again.

Ethiopia is also experiencing ongoing tension with Somalia to the east. Somalia has been an unstable country for many years and has been without a centralized government since 1991. The chaos led to our country's intervention in Somalia in 2006. We intervened to support the transitional government during that time, but our efforts were ineffective. Several thousand Ethiopians died in this conflict between the years 2006-2009. While our country's military has pulled out of Somalia as of January 2009, there are still ongoing threats of conflict again with Somalia.

Besides the fighting in recent years, our country has also unfortunately struggled with famine. While we have modernized substantially over the past hundred years, many in Ethiopia do subsistence farming. In other words, many farmers grow just enough food for their own families. They do not buy food in the market places or trade. So if there is a crop failure one year, then many are vulnerable to famine.

Unfortunately, we have had crop failures in the past due to lack of rain as well as poverty. We faced a severe famine in 1984-1985 that affected 8 million people and led to 1 million deaths.[33] Our country was helped by an event called Live Aid that donated thousands of dollars to help relieve famine or there would have been even more fatalities. Famine struck our country again in 2003. Tens of thousands died in this famine. Thanks to foreign aid millions were saved.[34] Famines once again threatened 6.2 million people in our land in 2009.[35] It is uncertain how many died in this famine.

While we have faced much suffering in our country, we still rejoice at Christmas time. There is a rich Christian history in Ethiopia, and we take great pleasure at Christmas time. Ethiopia declared itself a Christian country in the fourth century. Sixty percent of our country considers itself Christian.

We celebrate several days following December 25, and our celebration is very joyful. Nearly everyone celebrates in

---

[33] Patrick Webb and Joachim von Braun. *Famine and Food Security in Ethiopia: Lessons for Africa* (Chichester: John Wiley and Sons, 1994), 29.
[34] Roger Thurow, "For Generations, Politics kept Tributaries flowing by, bringing their Bounty to Egypt," *The Wall Street Journal* November 26, 2003, http://cindybeads.com/famine.htm (Accessed: May 29, 2011).
[35] "Millions facing Famine in Ethiopia as Rains fail," *The Independent Africa*, http://www.independent.co.uk/news/world/africa/millions-facing-famine-in-ethiopia-as-rains-fail-1779376.html (Accessed: May 29, 2011).

our country.  The main day for celebrating Christmas is December 29 because our calendar resembles the Egyptian Coptic calendar.

At Christmas time, people not only celebrate in church but publicly.  Many people appear on television giving congratulations to Christians.  Our television will also show reporters interviewing people on the streets.  These reporters will ask passersby, "What did you feel about Christmas Day?" or "How did you celebrate?" or "Did you buy any new clothes for Christmas Day?"  There are many interviews shown publicly during Christmas time.

The church where I serve, an Evangelical Lutheran church, celebrates in special ways.  The most important celebration is a special Christmas service in which children tell about the birth of Jesus.  In that service, the children will hold candles and read different parts of the Bible.  The joy on their faces is inspiring.

After church on Christmas Day, people go to eat with other church members in their homes.  Many of the homes will be decorated with natural flowers picked right from the field.  Many flowers grow at this time of year because the temperatures are right.  So, there are many flowers to be picked, particularly the Abyssian rose.

While many celebrate Christmas in Ethiopia, the part of Christmas that touches me most is Jesus' suffering.  Luke 2:6-7 moves me when I read it when it says,

> While they were there, the time came for the baby to be born, and she gave birth to her firstborn, a son. She wrapped him in cloths and placed him in a manger, because there was no room for them in the inn.

Jesus did not even have a proper place to be born although he was God. Mary and Joseph could find no room for him to be born as Luke 2 tells us. Instead, he was born in a manger, the place where they laid the food for the animals. He was wrapped in swaddling clothes and not princely robes.

Because Jesus was born in this way, it shows me that from the very beginning of his life, Jesus was suffering for me. Jesus not only suffered at his crucifixion but also from the very beginning of his life. Jesus lowered himself for me from the very beginning of his life because of my sin. It humbles me, and I am amazed and thankful for his sacrifice for me.

*A prayer request for Ethiopia:*

Pray for those who are vulnerable to famine in Ethiopia. Ask God for lasting solutions to this repeated problem of famine.

*Gemechis Chala*

# December 30:

# Democratic Republic

# of Congo –

# Giving out of Poverty

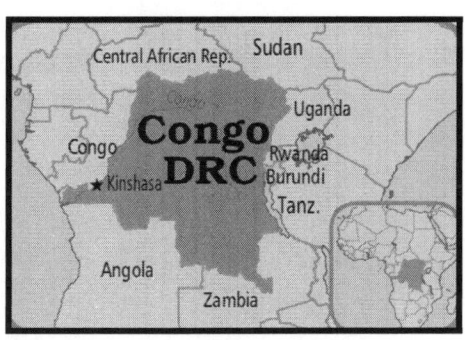

The Democratic Republic of Congo, formerly known as Zaire, stands right in the middle of the continent of Africa. It is the size of Western Europe and is the third largest country in Africa following Sudan and Algeria. There are approximately 71 million people in the country, and it is the most populous nation in French speaking Africa.

The Democratic Republic of Congo and also the center of the continent of Africa have had a great amount of conflict in recent years. In 1998 the Great War of Africa (also called the Second Congo War) started. It began in the Democratic Republic of Congo. While many in the West know less about this war, the fighting has involved eight African nations, resulting in the deaths of 5.4 million people. The fatalities in this war make it the deadliest conflict since the Second World War. As a result of this fighting, the Democratic Republic of Congo has suffered greatly.

Peace was declared in 2003, but fighting continues in the east of the country. This is the area where I lived for several years in the city of Bukavu. I was part of Tearfund's disaster prevention and management operation in eastern Congo.[36] Our goal was to bring God's Word of hope and light through practical deeds to the local population. I served with a team of missionaries in Bukavu.

There are about 250,000 people who live in that small city which is 10 km from the border of Rwanda. Some will be familiar with Rwanda due to the acclaimed film *Hotel Rwanda* (2004) that represented the Rwandan fighting between the Hutu and Tutsi people in the 1990s. Bukavu received many refugees from the fighting in Rwanda during that time.

Bukavu is a city which is in an advanced state of decay. The roads are steep and muddy and are in great need of repair. There are also thousands of small, mud huts which house most of the population. These huts accommodate an average family which has 6 children. These small huts lie also in dangerous areas where landslides often occur.

Besides the danger of mudslides, Bukavu is in danger due to the fighting that is still happening. The city is right in the middle of the Kivu conflict. While many do not know about this fighting, the Kivu conflict continues between the Democratic Forces for the Liberation of Rwanda (FDLR) and the military of the Democratic Republic of the Congo. The United Nations is also involved, trying to keep peace. Thousands have died as a result of this fighting and thousands more are refugees.

The arrival in Eastern Congo of several Rwandan ethnic groups just after the genocide in 1995 destabilized the region even more so. Agricultural activities were abandoned by most Congolese families because they feared the looting of their produce and the violence of the various armed groups. This resulted in extreme poverty and hunger for the local population.

---

[36] For further information on Tearfund, see http://www.tearfund.org/.

In eastern Congo, there has been a tremendous amount of sexual violence. It has been described by some as the worst in the world.[37] Rape has been used as a weapon to afflict innocent women and children in the area. Throughout the Democratic Republic of Congo, 200,000 women and children have been raped in 12 years of conflict according to UN estimates.[38]

Despite all of the problems in Bukavu, I was touched by something that happened at Christmas time in 2006. After a violent attack from militia on many innocent people living in neighboring villages, many were wounded and were brought to hospital in Bukavu. The local church pastor asked the population to gather rice, beans, and soap for the wounded. We all participated and spent the rest of Christmas Day wrapping gift parcels for those victims in hospital.

On Boxing Day (December 26) we went in groups of 5, distributing Christmas parcels throughout the wards, while reading passages from the Bible and singing Christmas carols. What was particularly noticeable was the generosity of the people. The gifts were gathered by local people of whom 90% live under the poverty line of 1 dollar per day. What a meaningful example of sharing and compassion!

This experience gives fresh meaning to a passage like 2 Corinthians 9:7 which reads, "Each man should give what he has decided in his heart to give, not reluctantly or under compulsion, for God loves a cheerful giver." May God help us all with generosity this Christmas time!

---

[37] Jeffrey Gettleman, "Rape Epidemic Raises Trauma of Congo War," New York Times, http://www.nytimes.com/2007/10/07/world/africa/07congo.html (Accessed: February 13, 2011).

[38] Maris Beck, "Rape is the Weapon of Choice," The Age, http://www.theage.com.au/world/in-congo-war-rape-is-the-weapon-of-choice-20081121-6e45.html (Accessed: February 13, 2011).

*A prayer request for the Democratic Republic of Congo:*

Please pray for peace and protection for people in the Democratic Republic of Congo. Pray against violence so that aid agencies can reach the millions of starving Rwandan, Burundian, and Congolese refugees.

*Tilly Leuring*

# December 31:

# Scotland – Obedience

# to God's Call

Scotland is north of England and is one of four countries that make up the United Kingdom. I come from the town of Milngavie, which has some 13,000 residents and lies north and west of Glasgow in western Scotland. Many in Milngavie commute to Glasgow for their work. If you follow football, you may be interested in knowing that the Scottish Football Club Rangers has a training facility in my town.

Scotland has been influenced by Christianity for centuries. The Christian faith came to Scotland in approximately 400 AD. It became firmly established in the sixth and seventh centuries and then more greatly connected with Roman Catholicism later on. Christmas was remembered in many ways during these years.

From the time of the Reformation in the sixteenth century, many stopped celebrating Christmas. This came about from the strong influence of Reformed teaching. In the sixteenth century, Scotland was bound by strong traditions that came from a corrupt church at that time. Many of the clergy were morally bankrupt and ignorant of the Scriptures. This also affected the Scottish people who did not hear the Scriptures and were led to worship in superstitious ceremonies and traditions. They were reading the Scriptures in a language that they did not understand, taught to pray to dead saints, and were sold indulgences for the forgiveness of their sins.

This all changed in the sixteenth century when the Reformation reached Scotland. Martyrs such as Patrick Hamilton initiated the Reformation. He was burned at the stake in Saint Andrews for calling the church in Scotland back to the Scriptures. Other influential people moved the Scottish church through their preaching such as George Wishart, and eventually John Knox who promoted the Reformation perspective. Knox was a particularly powerful preacher. He called the church back to the priority of the word of God and taught that all other traditions must be subject to the Scriptures.

Knox is also known for introducing something which is now called the regulative principle. This principle states that only what God has required in his word should be introduced into the worship of God. Knox applied this to teachings of the church regarding the pope, the mass, purgatory, and prayers to the dead. This principle was then applied to Christmas, too, as it was deemed to be a Catholic activity. Christmas observances were suppressed since there are no biblical commandments to celebrate Jesus' birth. In 1583, there was even a ban placed on celebrating Christmas; after this it was not celebrated until the twentieth century.[39]

With the importance of Christmas reduced, the celebration of New Year's Eve grew into a great tradition called "Hogmanay." It is celebrated on New Year's Eve and runs into New Year's Day and the day after. The most widespread tradition on New Year's Eve is "first footing," which starts immediately after midnight on New Years' Eve.

---

[39] For further information about the Scottish Reformation and its ongoing effects, see the Scottish Reformation Society website: http://www.scottishreformationsociety.org.uk/ or http://www.reformation-scotland.org.uk/scottish-reformation-society.php.

It is good luck for a family to be visited by a friend or neighbor at the stroke of midnight.  At that time, the visitor is supposed to give a symbolic gift such as salt, coal, wood, whisky, or shortbread.  "First footing" may go on throughout the early hours of the morning and well into the next day.

While Hogmanay is still the greater holiday, Christmas celebration has returned to Scotland.  Many Christians will attend a midnight service to see in Christmas and go to church on Christmas morning to start the day with worship.  Christmas is a time when family and friends will often give gifts to each other. For many families, apart from birthdays, Christmas is the time we give the most generous presents to each other.  Increasingly, however, Christmas is being seen as a winter festival, and there is less emphasis on the Christian meaning.  The emphasis with children is more on Santa Claus and not on Jesus.

No matter what place Christmas traditions have, there are still many aspects of the Christmas story which are found in the Bible that are valuable for us today.  For example, I am impressed by the way that Mary responds to the announcement of the angel Gabriel in Luke 1.  We read in Luke 1:35-38 the following:

> The angel answered, "The Holy Spirit will come upon you, and the power of the Most High will overshadow you. So the holy one to be born will be called the Son of God.  Even Elizabeth your relative is going to have a child in her old age, and she who was said to be barren is in her sixth month.  For nothing is impossible with God."  "I am the Lord's servant," Mary answered. "May it be to me as you have said." Then the angel left her.

What is particularly striking to me is her statement, "I am the Lord's servant, may it be to me as you have said."  It is exemplary obedience.

The Lord wants obedience for us at Christmas time as well as throughout the year. As Samuel said in 1 Samuel 15:22, "To obey is better than sacrifice." This is what he wants for Christians as we begin the New Year. May God help us to follow his word and not be caught up in traditions that would keep us from him!

*A prayer request for Scotland:*

Church attendance is declining in Scotland. Pray that Christian leaders will be faithful with God's word in the church. Also, pray that evangelism would increase in the United Kingdom.

*Alastair MacDonald*

# Afterword

## *One Minute of Prayer each day for the World*

God calls us to different stations in the world. Yet, he asks us to be responsible beyond our own needs.

The following are 7 suggested prayer requests for the world – one for each day of the week. Please consider praying for the needs in the world for one minute a day. James 5:16b reads, "The prayer of a righteous man is powerful and effective." There is no telling how great a difference can be made by sincere Christians praying for others.

**Sunday**: *Pray for the spread of the Christian message.* Pray for the development of international Christian leaders. Pray also for the work of Bible translation. Today approximately 350 million people do not have the Bible in their own language. For further news and testimonies, see the website of Tyndale Theological Seminary at www.tyndale-europe.edu and Wycliffe Bible translators at http://www.wycliffe.org.

**Monday**: *Pray for current events.* Read or listen to the international news and pray for particular events. For current international news see websites like: http://global.nytimes.com/ or www.bbc.co.uk.

**Tuesday**: *Pray for people who have never heard of Jesus Christ.* Of the world's 7 billion people, 2.74 billion have never heard of Jesus Christ. Ask God for laborers to go out into the harvest field (Rom 10:9-15). For further information see "The Joshua Project" website sponsored by the US Center for World Mission: http://www.joshuaproject.net.

**Wednesday**: *Pray for strength and perseverance for Christian believers who suffer for proclaiming Jesus Christ as Lord.* The top 10 countries where Christians are most persecuted are: North Korea, Iran, Saudi Arabia, Somalia, Maldives, Afghanistan, Yemen, Mauritania, Laos, and Uzbekistan. For further news on the persecuted church see the Voice of the Martyrs website at http://www.persecution.com or International Day of Prayer for the Persecuted Church at http://www.persecutedchurch.org.

**Thursday**: *Pray for Christianity's interaction with other world religions.* There are repeated clashes with Islam in places in Africa, Europe, and Asia. Christianity has also clashed with Hinduism and Buddhism in places in Asia. Pray for understanding and peace. Pray also against terrorism.

**Friday**: *Pray for one missionary that your church supports.* Pray for their devotional life, strength in their family, cultural adjustment, financial support, and faithfulness to the mission task that they have been given.

**Saturday**: *Pray for issues of world crisis.* HIV, poverty, shelter, and food. Pray for wisdom and resources to meet these crises. There are 1.02 billion people without enough food. There are 33 million living with HIV. Almost half the world lives on less than $2.50 per day. Pray for resources to reach those in need. Pray for wisdom amongst the international community to help those in need. Ask God to use the Christian church worldwide to meet these needs as it witnesses to Jesus Christ as Savior and Lord. For further information see: World Vision's website: http://www.wvi.org/wvi/wviweb.nsf or Samaritan's Purse: http://www.samaritanspurse.org.